Student Study Guide

D1145806

GLENCOE Aviation Technology Series

Aircraft
Powerplants

Seventh Edition

REFERENCE ONLY
Please do not remove
from the centre

Michael J. Kroes
Thomas W. Wild

GLENCOE
McGraw-Hill

New York, New York   Columbus, Ohio   Woodland Hills, California   Peoria, Illinois

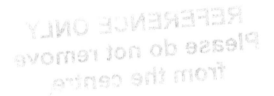
REFERENCE ONLY
Please do not remove
from the centre

Student Study Guide for Aircraft Powerplants, Seventh Edition

Imprint 2001
Copyright © 1995 by Glencoe/McGraw-Hill. All rights reserved. Except as permitted under the United States Copyright Act, no part of this publication may be
reproduced or distributed in any form or by any means, or stored in a database
or retrieval system, without prior permission of the publisher.

Send all inquiries to:
Glencoe/McGraw-Hill
8787 Orion Place
Columbus, OH 43240

ISBN 978-0-02-801875-1
MHID 0-02-801875-3

Printed in the United States of America.

11 12 13 14 15 16 17 18 19 20 QSR QSR 9

Contents

To the Student

This *Student Study Guide* has been developed to accompany the textbook *Aircraft Powerplants*, 7th Edition. Its purpose is to help the student reinforce his or her understanding of the principles and concepts covered in the text.

Each series of *Study Questions* is intended for the student to use after thoroughly reading the corresponding chapter. Many of the key points are covered in these questions to help the student review and better understand what he or she has read.

The *Application Questions* allow the student to apply basic principles and concepts or to interpret and use other information presented.

A *Review Exam* at the conclusion of each chapter provides a means of validating an adequate knowledge of the chapter material.

Although many of the key points from the text are covered in this *Study Guide*, it would have been impossible to include everything. The student should not attempt to use this material as a substitute for a thorough study of the textbook.

It is suggested that the user first read the related chapter in its entirety *before* attempting to complete the fill-in-the-blank (study) questions. In this way, the completion of the fill-in-the-blank questions will both act as a review and reinforce the significance of particular discussions in the text.

The application questions should then be completed to ensure that the topic is understood. In most cases, these questions will require that the principles and concepts covered in the study questions be applied to typical problems or systems. In some instances, questions relate to one another in order to demonstrate the interrelationships between different concepts. Completion of the application questions will further enhance the student's understanding of the chapter material.

Finally, for many users of this *Study Guide*, the primary objective will be the attainment of an Airman's Certificate with a Powerplant Rating. To assist in this effort, the *Study Guide* concludes each chapter with a review exam consisting of a scrics of multiple choice questions designed to represent those typically found in the FAA Powerplant Test.

Michael J. Kroes
Thomas W. Wild

Chapter 1

STUDY QUESTIONS

1. The cylinders of an in-line engine are arranged in a _____ row parallel to the crankshaft.

2. In an in-line engine there are generally an _____ number of cylinders in order to provide a proper balance of firing impulses.

3. The number of crankshafts in an in-line engine is _____ . The crankshaft(s) is (are) located above the cylinders in an _____ in-line engine.

4. In a V-type engine, the cylinders are arranged on the crankcase in two rows (or banks), forming the letter V, with an angle between the banks of _____ , _____ , or _____°. There are always an _____ number of cylinders in each row.

5. A single-row radial engine has an _____ number of cylinders extending radially from the centerline of the crankshaft.

6. The number of cylinders in a single-row radial engine usually ranges from _____ to _____ .

7. A double-row radial engine resembles two single-row radial engines combined on a single _____ .

8. The usual number of cylinders in a double-row radial engine is either _____ or _____ .

9. On a double-row radial engine, the cylinders in the rear row are located directly behind the spaces between the cylinders in the front row. This allows the cylinders in both rows to receive ram air for the necessary _____ .

10. The radial engine has the disadvantage of greater _____ because of the larger area presented to the air.

11. The largest and most powerful piston-type engine built and used successfully in the United States is the _____ .

12. The most popular engine for use in light conventional aircraft and helicopters is the _____ -type engine.

13. The opposed-type engine is usually mounted with the cylinders _____ .

14. Aircraft engines may be classified according to cylinder arrangement with respect to the crankshaft. List the different types of cylinder arrangements.

a. _____

b. _____

c. _____

d. _____

e. _____

f. _____

g. _____

h. _____

i. _____

j. _____

15. Aircraft engines may be classified as being cooled either by _____ or by _____ .

16. The first practical turbojet engines in England and the United States evolved from the work of _____ in England.

Chapter 1

APPLICATION QUESTIONS

1. List the different types of cylinder arrangements used in reciprocating engines.

   a. _____

   b. _____

   c. _____

   d. _____

2. Match the following engine characteristic letters with the definitions below.

   a. L _____

   b. T _____

   c. V _____

   d. H _____

   e. R _____

   f. O _____

   g. G _____

   h. S _____

   i. A _____

   j. I _____

   (1) Vertical, for helicopter installation with the crankshaft in a vertical position.
   (2) Turbocharged with turbine-operated device.
   (3) Left-hand rotation, for counterrotating propeller.
   (4) Horizontal, for helicopter installation with the crankshaft horizontal.
   (5) Aerobatic; fuel and oil systems designed for sustained inverted flight.
   (6) Fuel injected; continuous fuel injection system installed.
   (7) Geared nose section, for reduction of propeller revolutions per minute (rpm).
   (8) Supercharged; engine structurally capable of operating with high manifold pressure and equipped with either a turbine-driven supercharger or an engine-driven supercharger.
   (9) Opposed cylinders.
   (10) Radial engine; cylinders arranged radially around the crankshaft.

3. Define the following engine designations.

   a. IO-320

   _____

   b. GTSIO-520-E1B4D

   _____

   _____

   _____

4. Label the following engine cylinder arrangement diagrams.

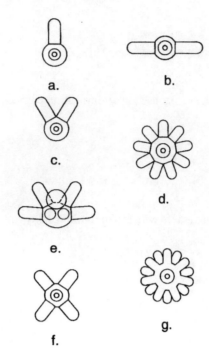

a.

b.

c.

d.

e.

f.

g.

a. _____

b. _____

c. _____

d. _____

e. _____

f. _____

g. _____

Chapter 1

Name _____

Date _____

REVIEW EXAM

1. GTSIO-520 indicates a geared
   a. supercharged, injected, opposed engine of 520 in³ displacement.
   b. turbosupercharged, injected, opposed engine of 520 in³ displacement.
   c. turbosupercharged, injected, opposed engine of 520 cm³ displacement.
   d. turbosupercharged, injected, opposed engine of 520 horsepower.

2. Heat is transferred to the air from the cooling fins by
   a. radiation.
   b. convection.
   c. induction.
   d. conduction.

3. An in-line engine cylinder arrangement is one in which the cylinders of the engine are
   a. arranged in the shape of a letter V.
   b. arranged in a single row parallel to the crankshaft.
   c. arranged in two rows perpendicular to the crankshaft.
   d. arranged in a circular pattern.

4. A single-row radial engine has
   a. an odd number of cylinders extending radially from the centerline of the crankshaft.
   b. an even number of cylinders extending parallel to the length of the crankshaft.
   c. an odd number of cylinders forming a straight line parallel to the length of the crankshaft.
   d. all of the above.

5. The first practical turbojet engine in England and the United States evolved from the work of
   a. the Wright brothers.
   b. George B. Brayton.
   c. Gottlieb Daimler.
   d. Frank Whittle.

Chapter 2

STUDY QUESTIONS

1. The part of an engine that comprises the housing which encloses the various mechanisms surrounding the crankshaft is the _____ .

2. Most aircraft engine crankcases are made of _____ because it is both light and strong.

3. The typical radial-engine crankcase has four major sections. These sections are the _____ , _____ , _____ , and _____ sections.

4. Any surface that supports or is supported by another surface is called a _____ .

5. Bearings which are designed primarily to take thrust loads are called _____ bearings.

6. Three general types of bearings are the _____ bearing, the _____ bearing, and the _____ bearing.

7. The component which transforms the reciprocating motion of the piston and connecting rod into rotary motion for turning the propeller is the _____ .

8. The principal parts of the crankshaft are the _____ , the _____ , the _____ , and the _____ .

9. The part of the crankshaft that is supported by and rotates in a main bearing is the _____ .

10. The purpose of a counterweight is to provide _____ for a crankshaft.

11. The purpose of _____ is to relieve the whip and vibration caused by the rotation of the crankshaft.

12. Aircraft engines are equipped with one of three types of propeller mounting shafts: _____ , _____ , or _____ .

13. The link which transmits forces between the piston and the crankshaft of an engine is the _____ .

14. The connecting rod furnishes the means of converting the _____ motion of the piston to a _____ movement of the crankshaft in order to drive the propeller.

15. The master and articulated connecting-rod assembly is used primarily for _____ engines.

16. The articulated rods (link rods) are hinged to the master rod flanges by means of steel _____ .

17. The _____ is a plunger that moves back and forth or up and down within an engine cylinder barrel.

18. Grooves are machined around the outer surface of the piston to provide support for the _____ .

19. The metal between the piston grooves is called a _____ .

20. Pistons may be classified according to the type of head used. The different types are _____ , _____ , _____ , _____ , and _____ .

21. List the three principal functions of piston rings.

    a. _____

    b. _____

    c. _____

22. Piston rings may be classified according to function as _____ rings and _____ rings.

23. The purpose of _____ rings is to prevent gases from escaping past the piston during engine operation.

24. The purpose of the _____ ring is to control the thickness of the oil film on the cylinder wall.

25. The rings placed on the skirts of the pistons to regulate the amount of oil passing between the piston skirts and cylinder walls during each of the piston strokes are the _____ rings.

26. A _____ pin, sometimes called a _____ pin, is used to attach the piston to the connecting rod.

27. The _____ of an internal-combustion engine converts the chemical heat energy of the fuel to mechanical energy and transmits it through pistons and connecting rods to the rotating crankshaft.

28. The two major units of the cylinder assembly are the cylinder _____ and the cylinder _____ .

29. The process whereby the nitrogen from anhydrous ammonia gas is forced to penetrate a steel surface is called _____ .

30. Cylinders which are bored with a slight taper are said to be _____ .

31. The _____ are cast or machined on the outside of the cylinder head in a pattern to provide the most efficient cooling and to take advantage of cylinder-head cooling baffles.

32. The main purpose of _____ in an internal-combustion engine is to open and close ports, which are openings into the combustion chamber of the engine.

33. The _____ are positioned to support and guide the stems of the valves.

34. A device for actuating the valve lifting mechanism is called a _____ .

35. A mechanism used to transmit the force of the cam to the valve pushrod is called a _____ .

36. A steel or aluminum-alloy rod or tube situated between the valve lifter and the rocker arm of the valve operating mechanism and used to transmit the motion of the valve lifter is the _____ .

37. The _____ is a pivoted arm mounted on bearings in the cylinder head and used to open and close the valves. One end of the arm presses on the _____ of the valve, and the other end receives motion from the _____ .

38. The cold clearance of the valves in an engine is usually much _____ than the "hot" (or operating) clearance.

39. The section of an engine which provides mounting pads for units such as the fuel pressure pumps, fuel injector pumps, vacuum pumps, oil pumps, tachometer generators, etc. is called the _____ .

40. The purpose of reduction gearing is to allow the _____ to rotate at the most efficient speed to absorb the power of the engine while the engine turns at a much higher rpm in order to develop full power.

Chapter 2

Name _____

Date _____

APPLICATION QUESTIONS

1. By means of a simple sketch, show the basic principles of operation of a dynamic balance.

2. Identify the following types of connecting-rod configurations and specify the type of engine in which each would be used.

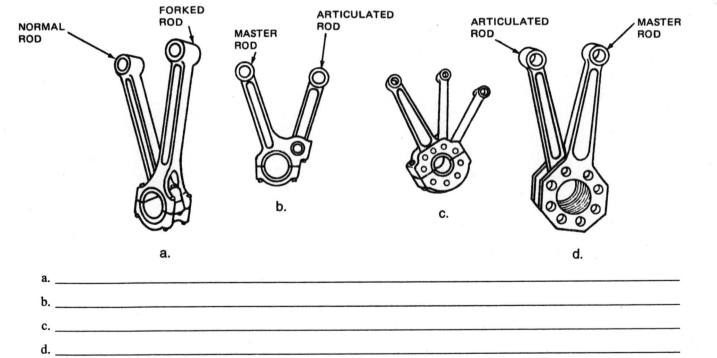

a. _____

b. _____

c. _____

d. _____

3. Identify the following types of piston configurations.

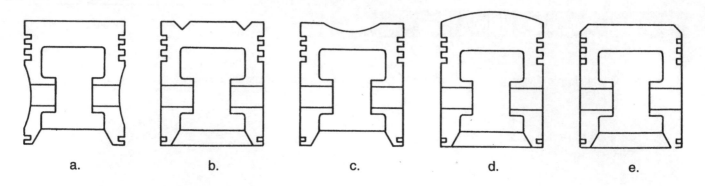

a.　　　　　　b.　　　　　　c.　　　　　　d.　　　　　　e.

a. _____

b. _____

c. _____

d. _____

e. _____

4. Identify the components of the valve train as shown in the diagram.

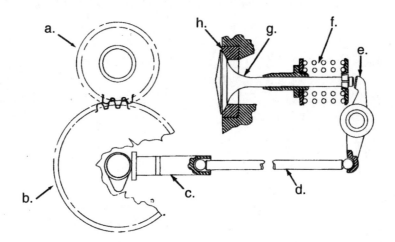

a. _____

b. _____

c. _____

d. _____

e. _____

f. _____

g. _____

h. _____

5. Label the following drawings showing the different arrangements for planetary reduction gear systems.

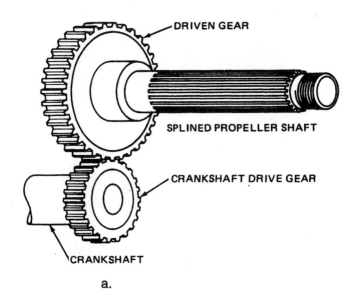

DRIVEN GEAR

SPLINED PROPELLER SHAFT

CRANKSHAFT DRIVE GEAR

CRANKSHAFT

a.

BELL GEAR STATIONARY   SUN GEAR ON CRANKSHAFT

BELL GEAR DRIVES PROPELLER SHAFT   SUN GEAR

BELL GEAR MOUNTED ON CRANKSHAFT   SUN GEAR STATIONARY

b.   c.   d.

a. _____

b. _____

c. _____

d. _____

Chapter 2

REVIEW EXAM

1. Which of the following statements is true regarding bearings used in high-powered reciprocating aircraft engines?
   a. The outer race of a single-row, self-aligning ball bearing will always have a radius equal to the radius of the balls.
   b. There is less rolling friction when ball bearings are used than when roller bearings are employed.
   c. Crankshaft bearings are generally of the ball type because of their ability to withstand extreme loads without overheating.
   d. Crankshaft bearings are generally of the ball type because of their ability to withstand loads. However, some manufacturers object to the use of ball bearings because they require a positive high-pressure oil supply.

2. Which propeller reduction-gear ratio will cause the highest propeller rpm? (Assume the same engine rpm in each case.)
   a. 16:7
   b. 16:9
   c. 20:9
   d. 3:2

3. Which of the following is the principal advantage of using propeller reduction gears?
   a. They enable the propeller rpm to be increased without an accompanying increase in engine rpm.
   b. They allow the diameter and blade area of the propeller to be increased.
   c. They permit the engine rpm to be increased with an accompanying increase in power and allow the propeller to remain at a lower, more efficient rpm.
   d. They enable the engine rpm to be increased with an accompanying increase in propeller rpm.

4. Which of the following is the type of thrust bearing used in most radial engines?
   a. Tapered roller
   b. Double-row ball
   c. Double-row straight roller
   d. Deep-groove ball

5. Which of the following bearings is least likely to be a roller or ball bearing?
   a. Rocker-arm bearing (overhead valve engine)
   b. Master rod bearing (radial engine)
   c. Crankshaft main bearing (radial engine)
   d. Generator armature bearing

6. The clearance between the rocker arm and the valve tip affects how many of the following?
   (1) Point at which valve opens
   (2) Height of valve opening
   (3) Duration of valve opening

   a. One
   b. Two
   c. Three
   d. None

7. Which of the following statements regarding engine crankshafts is true?
   a. Counterweights reduce torsional vibration.
   b. Counterweights provide static balance.
   c. A six-throw crankshaft utilizes three dynamic dampers.
   d. Dynamic dampers are designed to resonate at the natural frequency of the crankshaft.

8. Cam-ground pistons are installed in some aircraft engines to
   a. provide a better fit at operating temperature.
   b. cause the master rod piston to wear at the same rate as those installed on the articulating rods.
   c. act as a compensating feature so that a compensated magneto is not required.
   d. equalize the wear on pistons that do not operate in a vertical plane.

9. Some aircraft engine manufacturers equip their products with choked or taper-ground cylinders. Choke-type cylinders are used because they
   a. provide a straight cylinder bore at operating temperatures.
   b. reduce the possibility of piston rings sticking in the ring grooves.
   c. compensate for normal cylinder barrel wear.
   d. increase the compression pressure for starting purposes.

10. An overhead valve engine using zero-lash hydraulic valve lifters is observed to have no clearance in its valve operating mechanism after the minimum inlet-oil and cylinder-head temperatures for takeoff have been reached. This condition can be expected
    a. during normal operation.
    b. when the lifters become deflated.
    c. as a result of carbon and sludge becoming trapped in the lifter and restricting its motion.
    d. as a result of inverting the tappet valve during the assembly of the lifter.

11. The insides of some cylinder barrels are hardened by
    a. nitriding.
    b. shot peening.
    c. nickel plating.
    d. cadmium plating.

12. The operating valve clearance of an engine using hydraulic tappets (zero-lash lifters) should not exceed
    a. 0.15 to 0.18 in.
    b. 0.00 in.
    c. 0.25 to 0.32 in.
    d. 0.30 to 1.10 in.

13. Full floating piston pins are those which allow motion between the pin and
    a. the connecting rod.
    b. the piston.
    c. both the piston and the large end of the connecting rod.
    d. both the piston and the small end of the connecting rod.

14. The purpose of two or more valve springs in an aircraft engine is to
    a. reduce valve stretch.
    b. equalize side pressure on the valve stems.
    c. eliminate valve-spring surge.
    d. eliminate valve-stem breakage.

15. Consider the following statements:
    (1) Only cast-iron piston rings can be used in nitrided or chromium-plated cylinders.
    (2) Chromium-plated piston rings may be used in plain steel cylinders.
    Of these two statements,

    a. only No. 1 is true.
    b. only No. 2 is true.
    c. neither No. 1 nor No. 2 is true.
    d. both No. 1 and No. 2 are true.

16. Excessive valve clearance causes the valves to
    a. open early and close early.
    b. open late and close early.
    c. open early and close late.
    d. open late and close late.

17. An advantage of using metallic sodium–filled exhaust valves in aircraft reciprocating engines is
    a. increased resistance to corrosive gases.
    b. increased strength and resistance to fatigue.
    c. reduced valve operating temperatures.
    d. greater resistance to detonation at high valve temperatures.

18. Valve clearance changes on opposed-type engines using hydraulic lifters are accomplished by
    a. rocker-arm adjustment.
    b. rocker-arm replacement.
    c. adding or removing valve-stem shims.
    d. pushrod replacement.

19. The source of most of the heat that is absorbed by the lubricating oil in a reciprocating engine is the
    a. connecting-rod bearings.
    b. crankshaft main bearings.
    c. exhaust valves.
    d. pistons and cylinder walls.

20. The way in which the oil collected by the piston ring is returned to the crankcase is
    a. down vertical slots cut in the piston wall between the piston oil ring groove and the piston skirt.
    b. through hollow piston pins.
    c. through holes drilled in the piston oil ring groove.
    d. through holes drilled in the piston-pin recess.

Chapter 3

1. The capacity for doing work is called _____ .

2. Boyle's law states that the volume of any dry gas varies _____ with the absolute pressure sustained by it, the temperature remaining _____ .

3. Charles' law states that the pressure of a confined gas is directly proportional to its _____ .

4. An engine _____ is the series of events that an internal-combustion engine goes through while it is operating and delivering power.

5. In a four-stroke five-event cycle, these events are _____ , _____ , _____ , _____ , and _____ .

6. The four-stroke five-event cycle is called the _____ cycle.

7. The basic power-developing parts of a typical gasoline engine are the _____ , _____ , _____ , and _____ .

8. The distance through which the piston travels is called the _____ .

9. During each stroke, the crankshaft rotates _____ °.

10. _____ may be defined as the point which a piston has reached when it is at its maximum distance from the centerline of the crankshaft.

11. The _____ of a cylinder is the ratio of the volume of space in the cylinder when the piston is at the bottom of its stroke to the volume when the piston is at the top of its stroke.

12. In a four-stroke-cycle engine, the crankshaft makes _____ r for each complete cycle.

13. Ignition is caused by a _____ which produces an electric spark in the fuel-air mixture.

14. The ignition is timed to occur a few degrees _____ to allow time for complete combustion of the fuel.

15. During the _____ stroke, both valves are closed, the piston moves toward TDC, compressing the fuel-air mixture, and ignition takes place near the top of the stroke.

16. During the _____ stroke, the intake valve is open and the exhaust valve is closed, the piston moves downward, drawing the fuel-air mixture into the cylinder, and the intake valve closes.

17. During the _____ stroke, the exhaust valve is open and the intake valve is closed, the piston moves toward TDC, forcing the burned gases out through the open exhaust valve, and the intake valve opens near the top of the stroke.

18. During the _____ stroke, both valves are closed, the pressure of the expanding gases forces the piston toward BDC, and the exhaust valve opens well before the bottom of the stroke.

19. The angular distance through which both valves are open is called _____ .

20. The exhaust valve opens before BC for two principal reasons: more thorough _____ of the cylinder and better _____ of the engine.

21. The opening or closing of the intake or exhaust valves after TC or BC is called _____ .

22. The opening or closing of the intake or exhaust valves before BC or TC is called _____ .

23. The order in which the engine cylinders fire is called the _____ .

24. _____ is the rate of doing work.

25. One horsepower equals _____ ft·lb/min.

26. The _____ of one piston is obtained by multiplying the area of a cross section of the cylinder bore by the total distance that the piston moves during one stroke in the cylinder.

27. The horsepower developed by the engine—that is, the total horsepower converted from heat energy to mechanical energy—is the _____ horsepower.

28. The actual horsepower delivered by an engine to a propeller or other driven device is _____ horsepower.

29. That part of the total horsepower necessary to overcome the friction of the moving parts in the engine and its accessories is called _____ horsepower.

30. The pressure of the fuel-air mixture in the intake manifold between the carburetor or internal supercharger and the intake valve is the _____ .

31. The maximum continuous power is also called the _____ .

32. The greatest power output that the engine can develop at any time under any condition is called _____ power.

33. The highest level at which an engine will maintain a given horsepower output is the _____ altitude.

34. The measure of the heat losses suffered in converting the heat energy of the fuel to mechanical work is _____ efficiency.

35. The efficiency of an engine is the ratio of _____ to _____ .

36. The ratio of the volume of the fuel-air charge burned by the engine at atmospheric pressure and temperature to the piston displacement is the _____ efficiency.

37. A naturally aspirated (unsupercharged) engine always has a volumetric efficiency of less than _____ percent.

38. Detonation will result whenever the _____ and _____ in the cylinder become excessive.

39. _____ is caused when there is a hot spot in the engine that ignites the fuel-air mixture before the spark plug fires.

40. The number of pounds of fuel burned per hour for each bhp produced is the _____ .

41. The best _____ mixture for an aircraft engine is that fuel-air mixture which permits the engine to develop maximum power at a particular rpm.

42. The best _____ mixture is that fuel-air mixture which provides the lowest bsfc.

Chapter 3

APPLICATION QUESTIONS

1. By means of a simple sketch, show or define engine bore and stroke.

2. What is the compression ratio of the cylinder shown in the diagram below? _____

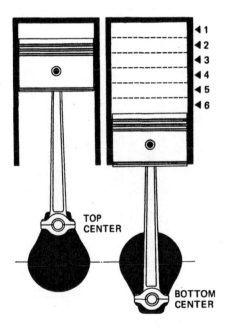

3. Label the four strokes of the four-stroke engine in the diagram.

FUEL-AIR MIXTURE INLET

INTAKE VALVE OPENS

INTAKE VALVE CLOSES

(A)

COMBUSTION STARTS

INTAKE VALVE CLOSES

EXHAUST VALVE OPENS

(B)

(C)

EXHAUST GAS OUTLET

EXHAUST VALVE CLOSES

EXHAUST VALVE OPENS

(D)

a. _____

b. _____

c. _____

d. _____

4. Define the valve timing abbreviations listed.
   a. ABC

   _____

   b. ATC

   _____

   c. BBC

   _____

   d. BC

   _____

   e. BDC

   _____

   f. BTC

   _____

   g. EC

   _____

   h. EO

   _____

   i. IC

   _____

   j. IO

   _____

   k. TC

   _____

   l. TDC

   _____

5. Using the valve timing diagram shown, answer the following questions.

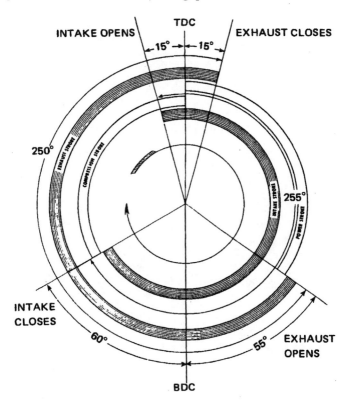

a. What is the duration in degrees of the total intake valve opening (actual intake stroke)?

_____

b. What is the total valve overlap?

_____

c. What is the duration in degrees of the total exhaust valve opening (actual exhaust stroke)?

_____

d. What is the actual duration of the compression stroke in degrees?

_____

e. What is the actual duration of the power stroke?

_____

6. Solve the following piston displacement problems.

Formula: Displacement = $0.7854 \times \text{bore}^2 \times \text{stroke} \times \text{number of cylinders}$

a. Bore = 5.125 in; stroke = 4.375 in; 6 cylinders:

Displacement = _____ in^3

b. Bore = 4.125 in; stroke = 6 in; 4 cylinders:

Displacement = _____ in^3

c. Bore = 5.125 in; stroke = 5.125 in; 8 cylinders:

Displacement = _____ in^3

7. Solve the following brake horsepower problems.

Formula: $\text{bhp} = \dfrac{F \times L \times 2\pi \times \text{rpm}}{33,000}$

a. F (force) = 200 lb; L (length of arm) = 4 ft; rpm = 1800:

bhp = _____

b. F = 400 lb; L = 4 ft; rpm = 2200:

bhp = _____

c. F = 150 lb; L = 4 ft; rpm = 2400:

bhp = _____

8. Solve the following indicated horsepower problems.

Formula: $\text{ihp} = \dfrac{PLANK}{33,000}$

a. P (imep) = 300 psi; L (length of stroke) = 0.5 ft; A (area of piston) = 76 in^2; N (actual engine rpm divided by 2) = 1500; K (number of cylinders) = 6:

ihp = _____

b. P = 200 psi; L = 0.4 ft; A = 80 in^2; N = 1200 rpm; K = 4:

ihp = _____

9. Solve the following brake thermal efficiency problems.

Formula: $\text{bte} = \dfrac{\text{bhp} \times 33,000}{\text{fuel burned (lb/min)} \times \text{heat value (Btu)} \times 778}$

a. bhp = 104; fuel burned = 6.5 gal/h (convert to lb/min); heat value = 20,000 Btu:

bte = _____ , or _____ %

b. bhp = 200; fuel burned = 8 gal/h (convert to lb/min); heat value = 20,000 Btu:

bte = _____ , or _____ %

Name _____

Date _____

10. Using Figure 3–15 on page 56 in the textbook, complete each statement below by indicating whether the likelihood of detonation will increase or decrease.

   a. If the compression ratio is increased, the likelihood of detonation will _____ .

   b. If the fuel-air mixture is leaned, the likelihood of detonation will _____ .

   c. If the air inlet temperature is decreased, the likelihood of detonation will _____ .

   d. If the engine is equipped with a high degree of supercharging, the likelihood of detonation will

      _____ .

   e. If the octane of the fuel is decreased, the likelihood of detonation will _____ .

   f. If the load on the engine is increased while the engine rpm is held constant, the likelihood of detonation will

      _____ .

11. Describe the difference between detonation and preignition.

   _____

   _____

   _____

12. Using the chart below, convert a pressure altitude of 10,000 ft at +90°F to density altitude.

   Density altitude = _____ ft

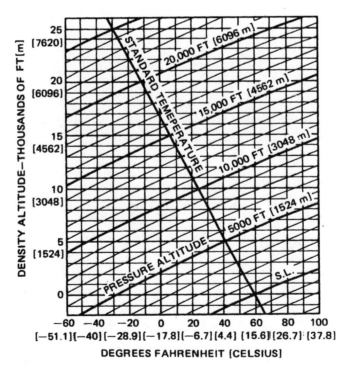

13. Use the charts below to answer the following questions.

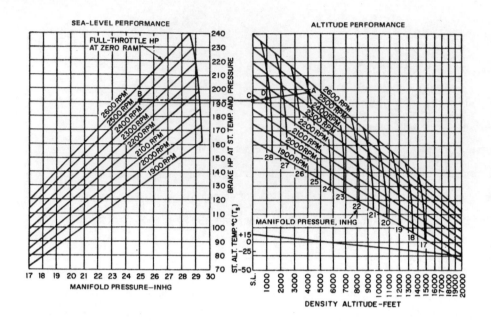

a. What is the horsepower being developed by an engine operating at 25 inHg and 2500 rpm at a density altitude of 1000 ft? _____

b. What is the horsepower being developed by an engine operating at 26 inHg and 2600 rpm at a density altitude of 10,000 ft? _____

14. Explain the effect of exhaust back pressure on engine performance.

_____

_____

Chapter 3

REVIEW EXAM

1. Which of the following will decrease volumetric efficiency of a reciprocating engine?
   a. High fuel octane rating
   b. Short intake pipes of large diameter
   c. Low carburetor air temperature
   d. High cylinder-head temperature

2. The horsepower developed in the cylinders of a reciprocating engine is known as
   a. shaft horsepower.
   b. indicated horsepower.
   c. brake horsepower.
   d. thrust horsepower.

3. A nine-cylinder engine with a bore of 5.5 in and a stroke of 6 in will have a total piston displacement of
   a. 740 in^3.
   b. 1425 in^3.
   c. 23,758 in^3.
   d. 1283 in^3.

4. The five events of a four-stroke-cycle engine in the order of their occurrence are
   a. intake, ignition, compression, power, and exhaust.
   b. intake, power, compression, ignition, and exhaust.
   c. intake, compression, ignition, power, and exhaust.
   d. intake, ignition, power, compression, and exhaust.

5. The primary concern in establishing the firing order for an opposed engine is to
   a. provide for balance and eliminate vibration to the greatest extent possible.
   b. achieve the highest cruising speed torque.
   c. keep power impulses on adjacent cylinders as far apart as possible in order to obtain the greatest mechanical efficiency.
   d. keep the power impulses on adjacent cylinders as close together as possible in order to obtain the greatest mechanical efficiency.

6. If the fuel-air ratio is proper and ignition timing is correct, the combustion process should
   a. be completed 20 to 30° before top center at the end of the compression stroke.
   b. be completed when the exhaust valve opens at the end of the power stroke.
   c. continue until the end of the exhaust stroke.
   d. be completed just after top center of the beginning of the power stroke.

7. On which stroke or strokes are both valves on a four-stroke-cycle reciprocating engine cylinder open?
   a. Exhaust
   b. Intake
   c. Power and intake
   d. Exhaust and intake

8. The actual power delivered to the propeller of an aircraft engine is called
   a. friction horsepower.
   b. brake horsepower.
   c. mechanical efficiency.
   d. indicated horsepower.

9. Using the following information, determine how many degrees the crankshaft will rotate with both the intake and exhaust valves seated: Intake opens 15° BTC; exhaust opens 70° BBC; intake closes 45° ABC; exhaust closes 10° ATC.
   a. 610°
   b. 290°
   c. 245°
   d. 25°

10. If the intake valve is opened too early in the operation of a four-stroke-cycle engine, it may result in
    a. improper scavenging of exhaust gases.
    b. engine kickback.
    c. backfiring into the induction system.
    d. incomplete compression.

11. Which of the following statements regarding a four-stroke-cycle aircraft engine is true?
    a. The intake valve closes on the compression stroke.
    b. The exhaust valve opens on the exhaust stroke.
    c. The intake valve opens on the intake stroke.
    d. The exhaust valve closes on the exhaust stroke.

12. When is the fuel-air mixture ignited in a conventional reciprocating engine?
    a. When the piston has reached top dead center of the intake stroke.
    b. Just as the piston begins the power stroke.
    c. Shortly before the piston reaches the top of the compression stroke.
    d. When the piston reaches top dead center of the compression stroke.

13. Ignition occurs at 28° BTC on a certain four-stroke-cycle engine, and the intake valve opens at 15° BTC. How many degrees of crankshaft travel after ignition does the intake valve open? (Consider one cylinder only.)
    a. 707°
    b. 373°
    c. 347°
    d. 13°

14. Valve overlap is defined as the number of degrees of crankshaft travel
    a. during which both valves are off their seats.
    b. between the closing of the intake valve and the opening of the exhaust valve.
    c. during which both valves are on their seats.
    d. between the closing of the exhaust valve and the opening of the intake valve.

15. If the exhaust valve of a four-stroke-cycle engine is closed and the intake valve is just closing, the piston is on the
    a. intake stroke.
    b. power stroke.
    c. exhaust stroke.
    d. compression stroke.

16. Compression ratio is the ratio between
    a. piston travel on the compression stroke and piston travel on the intake stroke.
    b. combustion chamber pressure on the combustion stroke and combustion chamber pressure on the exhaust stroke.
    c. cylinder volume with piston at bottom dead center and cylinder volume with piston at top dead center.
    d. fuel and air in the combustion chamber.

17. The volume of a cylinder equals 70 in³ when the piston is at bottom center. When the piston is at the top of the cylinder, the volume equals 10 in³. What is the compression ratio?
    a. 10:7
    b. 1:7
    c. 7:10
    d. 7:1

18. What is the firing order for a nine-cylinder radial engine?
    a. 1, 2, 3, 4, 5, 6, 7, 8, 9.
    b. 1, 2, 3, 8, 4, 7, 5, 6, 9.
    c. 1, 3, 5, 7, 9, 2, 4, 6, 8.
    d. 9, 4, 2, 7, 5, 6, 8, 1, 3.

19. Consider the following statements:
    (1) Preignition is caused by improper ignition timing.
    (2) Detonation occurs when an area of the combustion chamber becomes incandescent and ignites the fuel/air mixture in advance of the normal ignition.
    Of these two statements,

    a. only No. 1 is true.
    b. only No. 2 is true.
    c. both No. 1 and No. 2 are true.
    d. neither No. 1 nor No. 2 is true.

20. Which of the following conditions would be most likely to lead to detonation?
    a. Improper ignition timing
    b. Improper valve grinding at overhaul
    c. Use of fuel with an excessive octane rating
    d. Use of fuel with an insufficient octane rating

21. Which of the following conditions will increase the likelihood of detonation?
    (1) High manifold pressure
    (2) High intake air temperature
    (3) Engine overheating
    (4) Late ignition timing

    a. 1 and 4
    b. 3 and 4
    c. 1, 2, and 3
    d. 1, 2, 3, and 4

22. Which of the following statements regarding the volumetric efficiency of an engine is true?
    a. The volumetric efficiency of an engine will remain the same regardless of the amount of throttle opening.
    b. It is impossible to exceed 100% volumetric efficiency of any engine regardless of the type of supercharger used.
    c. Manifold pressure will increase as altitude horsepower is increased.
    d. It is possible to exceed 100% volumetric efficiency of some engines by the use of internal superchargers of the proper type.

23. The greatest portion of heat generated by combustion in a typical reciprocating aircraft engine is
    a. converted into useful power.
    b. removed by the oil system.
    c. carried out with the exhaust gases.
    d. dissipated through the cylinder walls and heads.

24. Which of the following results in a decrease in volumetric efficiency?
    a. Insufficient cylinder-head temperature
    b. Insufficient carburetor air temperature
    c. Part-throttle operation
    d. Short intake pipes of large diameter

25. Increased engine heat will cause volumetric efficiency to
    a. remain the same.
    b. decrease or increase depending on the engine rpm.
    c. decrease.
    d. increase.

Chapter 4

STUDY QUESTIONS

1. Any natural or artificial substance having greasy or oily properties which can be used to reduce friction between moving parts or to prevent rust and corrosion on metallic surfaces is called a _____ .

2. _____ is the weight of any substance compared with the weight of an equal volume of a standard substance.

3. The temperature to which oil must be heated in order to give off enough vapor to form a combustible mixture above the surface that will momentarily flash or burn when the vapor is brought into contact with a very small flame is called the _____ .

4. The fluid friction (or the body) of a liquid is called the _____ .

5. The viscosity _____ is an arbitrary measure of the rate of change in the viscosity of an oil with changes in temperature.

6. An aircraft engine oil must have _____ stability against oxidation, thermal cracking, and coking. It must also have _____ stability with regard to pressure and temperature.

7. When one surface slides over another, the interlocking particles of metal on each surface offer a resistance to motion known as _____ friction.

8. When a cylinder or sphere rolls over the surface of a plane object, the resistance to motion offered by the surfaces to each other is known as _____ friction.

9. Most aircraft oils other than straight mineral oils contain a _____ that suspends contaminants such as carbon, lead compounds, and dirt.

10. _____ oils react better to temperature changes than do _____ -grade oils.

11. The purpose of a _____ system is to supply oil to the engine at the correct pressure and volume to provide adequate lubrication and cooling for all parts of the engine which are subject to the effects of friction.

12. In a _____ lubrication system, a mechanical pump supplies oil under pressure to the bearings.

13. The oil temperature _____ is designed to maintain the temperature of the oil in an operating engine at the correct level.

14. The oil flow through the cooling portion of the oil temperature regulator is controlled by the oil cooler _____ valve.

15. The purpose of an oil pressure _____ is to control and limit the lubricating system oil pressure.

16. The purpose of an _____ is to remove solid particles of foreign matter from the oil before it enters the engine.

17. A _____ oil filter is positioned between the oil pump and the engine bearings, thereby filtering all the circulated oil of any contaminants before it is passed through the bearing surfaces.

18. During the inspection of the engine oil filter, the residue on the screens, disks, or disposable filter cartridge and the residue in the filter housing are carefully examined for _____ particles.

19. An oil _____ is usually placed in the discharge line from a vacuum pump or air pump, and its function is to remove the oil from the discharge air.

20. The oil gage line, which is connected to the system near the outlet of the engine pressure pump, is filled with _____ -viscosity oil in cold weather to obtain a true indication of the oil pressure during engine warm-up.

21. A restricting _____ is placed in the oil gage line to retain the low-viscosity oil and to prevent damage from pressure surges.

22. Oil pressure pumps may be of either the _____ type or the _____ type.

23. The scavenge pump for a dry-sump lubrication system or turbocharger is designed with a capacity _____ than that of the pressure pump.

24. In a _____ -sump engine, the lubricating oil for the engine is stored in the sump, which is attached to the lower side of the engine.

25. In a _____ -sump system, the oil is pumped out of the engine into an external oil tank.

Chapter 4

Name _____

Date _____

APPLICATION QUESTIONS

1. List the functions of engine oil.

    a. _____

    b. _____

    c. _____

    d. _____

    e. _____

    f. _____

2. Define the term "straight mineral oil."

    _____

    _____

    _____

3. Define the term "ashless dispersant oil."

    _____

    _____

    _____

4. Define the term "multiviscosity oil."

    _____

    _____

    _____

5. Explain the functions of an oil pressure relief valve.

    _____

    _____

    _____

6. Define the term "wet-sump lubrication system."

    _____

    _____

    _____

7. Define the term "dry-sump lubrication system."

    _____

    _____

    _____

Chapter 4

Name _____

Date _____

REVIEW EXAM

1. The indicated oil pressure of a particular dry-sump aircraft engine is higher at cruise rpm than at idle rpm. This indicates
   a. defective piston oil control rings.
   b. excessive relief valve spring tension.
   c. an insufficient oil supply.
   d. normal operation.

2. If the oil pressure of an engine is higher when the engine is cold than it is at normal operating temperatures,
   a. the oil system relief valve should be readjusted.
   b. the engine's lubrication system is probably operating normally.
   c. the oil dilution system should be turned on immediately.
   d. the engine should be shut down immediately.

3. What will be the result of operating an engine at extremely high temperatures using a lubricant recommended by the manufacturer for much lower temperatures?
   a. The oil pressure will be higher than normal.
   b. The oil pressure gage will fluctuate excessively.
   c. The oil temperature and oil pressure will be higher than normal.
   d. The oil pressure will be lower than normal.

4. An oil separator is generally associated with which of the following?
   a. Engine-driven oil pressure pump
   b. Engine-driven vacuum pump
   c. Cuno oil filter
   d. Strainer-type filter

5. The time in seconds required for exactly 60 cm³ of oil to flow through an accurately calibrated orifice at a specific temperature is recorded as a measurement of the oil's
   a. flash point.
   b. specific gravity.
   c. viscosity.
   d. pour point.

6. The viscosity of a liquid is a measure of its
   a. resistance to flow.
   b. rate of change of internal friction with change in temperature.
   c. density.
   d. ability to transmit force.

7. An engine's lubricating oil aids in reducing friction, cushioning shock, and
   a. cooling the engine.
   b. preventing fatigue of engine parts.
   c. heating fuel in the carburetor to prevent icing.
   d. preventing a buildup of internal pressures in the crankcase.

8. Which of the following factors determines the proper grade of oil to use in a particular engine?
   a. Sufficient viscosity to provide good flow characteristics
   b. Adequate lubrication in various attitudes of flight
   c. Positive introduction of oil to the bearings
   d. Operating speeds of bearings

9. Specific gravity is a comparison of the weight of a substance to the weight of an equal volume of
   a. oil at a specific temperature.
   b. distilled water at a specific temperature.
   c. mercury at a specific temperature.
   d. isopropyl at a specific temperature.

10. Which of the following has the greatest effect on the viscosity of lubricating oil?
    a. Temperature
    b. Oiliness
    c. Pressure
    d. Volatility

11. Lubricants may be classified according to their origins. Satisfactory aircraft engine lubricants are
    a. mineral or synthetic based.
    b. animal, vegetable, mineral, or synthetic based.
    c. vegetable, mineral, or synthetic based.
    d. animal, mineral, or synthetic based.

12. What type of oil do most engine manufacturers recommend for new reciprocating engine break-in?
    a. Metallic-ash detergent oil
    b. Ashless dispersant oil
    c. Straight mineral oil
    d. Semisynthetic oil

13. What type of oil do most engine manufacturers recommend after new reciprocating engine break-in?
    a. Metallic-ash detergent oil
    b. Ashless dispersant oil
    c. Straight mineral oil
    d. Metallic-ash synthetic oil

14. The engine oil temperature regulator is usually located between which of the following in a dry-sump engine?
    a. The engine oil supply pump and the internal lubrication system
    b. The scavenge pump outlet and the oil storage tank
    c. The oil storage tank and the engine oil supply pump
    d. The sumps and the scavenge pump inlet

15. In a reciprocating engine oil system, the temperature bulb senses oil temperature
    a. and indicates the average oil temperature.
    b. at a point after the oil has passed through the oil cooler.
    c. while the oil is in the hottest area of the engine.
    d. immediately before the oil enters the oil cooler.

16. What prevents pressure within the lubricating oil tank from rising above or falling below ambient pressure (reciprocating engine)?
    a. Oil tank check valve
    b. Oil pressure relief valve
    c. Oil tank vent
    d. Thermostatic bypass valve

17. What unit in an aircraft engine lubrication system is adjusted to maintain the desired system pressure?
    a. Oil pressure relief valve
    b. Oil filter bypass valve
    c. Oil pump
    d. Oil pressure indicator

18. In order to relieve excessive pump pressure in an engine's internal oil system, most engines are equipped with a
    a. vent.
    b. bypass valve.
    c. breather.
    d. relief valve.

19. What is the purpose of the check valve generally used in a dry-sump lubrication system?
    a. To prevent the oil from the oil temperature regulator from returning to the crankcase during inoperative periods
    b. To prevent the scavenge pump from losing its prime
    c. To prevent the oil from the supply tank from seeping into the crankcase during inoperative periods
    d. To prevent the oil from the pressure pump from entering the scavenge system

20. Cylinder walls are usually lubricated by
    a. splashed or sprayed oil.
    b. a direct-pressure system fed through the crankshaft, connecting rods, and piston pins to the oil control ring groove in the piston.
    c. oil that is picked up by the oil control ring when the piston is at bottom center.
    d. oil migration past the rings during the intake stroke.

21. If a full-flow oil filter is used on an aircraft engine, and the filter becomes clogged,
    a. the pressure buildup in the filter will collapse the screen and close off the oil supply to the engine.
    b. the oil will be bypassed to the magnetic oil sump plug where metallic particles will be removed.
    c. the oil will be bypassed back to the oil tank hopper where sediment and foreign matter will settle out prior to passage through the engine.
    d. the bypass valve will open and the oil pump will supply unfiltered oil to the engine.

22. What is the primary reason for changing aircraft engine lubricating oil at predetermined periods?
    a. The oil gradually becomes too thick.
    b. The oil becomes diluted with gasoline washing past the pistons into the crankcase.
    c. The oil becomes contaminated with moisture, acids, and finely divided suspended solid particles.
    d. Exposure to heat and oxygen causes a decreased ability to maintain a film under load.

23. The purpose of the flow control valve in a reciprocating engine oil system is to
    a. direct oil through or around the oil cooler.
    b. deliver cold oil to the hopper tank.
    c. relieve excessive pressure in the oil cooler.
    d. compensate for volumetric increases resulting from foaming of the oil.

24. Why are all oil tanks equipped with vent lines?
    a. To prevent pressure buildup in the engine
    b. To eliminate foaming in the tank
    c. To prevent pressure buildup in the tank
    d. To eliminate foaming in the engine

25. The pumping capacity of the scavenge pump in a dry-sump aircraft engine's lubrication system
    a. is greater than the capacity of the oil supply pump.
    b. is less than the capacity of the oil supply pump.
    c. is usually equal to the capacity of the oil supply pump in order to maintain constant oiling conditions.
    d. varies according to the oil supply tank capacity and not according to the oil supply pump capacity.

26. In which of the following situations will the oil cooler automatic bypass valve be open the greatest amount?
    a. Engine oil at normal operating temperature
    b. Engine oil above normal operating temperature
    c. Engine oil below normal operating temperature
    d. Engine stopped with no oil flowing after run-up

27. What will result if an oil filter screen becomes completely blocked?
    a. Oil will flow at 75% of the normal rate through the system.
    b. Oil flow to the engine will stop.
    c. Oil flow from the engine will stop.
    d. Oil will flow at the normal rate through the system.

28. In a reciprocating engine, oil is directed from the pressure relief valve to the inlet side of the
    a. scavenge pump.
    b. thermostatic control.
    c. oil temperature regulator.
    d. pressure pump.

29. If the oil in the oil cooler core and annular jacket becomes congealed, what unit prevents damage to the cooler?
    a. Baffle plates
    b. Oil pressure relief valve
    c. Airflow control valve bellows
    d. Surge protection valve

30. The main oil filters strain the oil at which point in the system?
    a. Immediately after it leaves the scavenge pump
    b. Immediately before it enters the pressure pump
    c. Just before it passes through the spray nozzles
    d. Just as it leaves the pressure pump

Chapter 5

STUDY QUESTIONS

1. The complete induction system for an aircraft engine includes three principal sections:

   a. _____

   b. _____

   c. _____

2. The ducting system for a nonsupercharged (naturally aspirated) engine comprises four principal parts:

   a. _____

   b. _____

   c. _____

   d. _____

3. The induction _____ is installed at or near the air scoop for the purpose of removing dirt, abrasive particles, sand, and even larger foreign materials before they are carried into the engine.

4. There are basically three types of induction air filters: _____ filters, _____ filters, and _____ filters.

5. The _____ air valve is used for the purpose of allowing air to flow to the engine if the air filter or other parts of the induction system should become clogged.

6. The _____ air valve is a gate which closes the main air duct and opens the duct to the heater muff when the control is on.

7. Small induction system leaks have the most noticeable effects at low rpm because the pressure differential between the atmosphere and the inside of the intake manifold _____ as rpm _____ .

8. Induction system icing is generally classified in three types: _____ ice, _____ ice, and _____ ice.

9. _____ and _____ allow an engine to develop maximum power for operation at high altitudes or for boosting engine power on takeoff.

10. Superchargers can be driven either by gearing from the _____ or by _____ gases.

11. A turbocharger that boosts the intake air pressure above 30 inHg [101.61 kPa] is called a _____ .

12. At altitudes above sea level, the pressure, density, and temperature of the air are _____ .

13. MAP is the pressure in the _____ of the engine.

14. In a normally aspirated engine, MAP is _____ than outside atmospheric pressure because of the air friction losses in the air induction system.

15. If MAP is too high, _____ and overheating will occur.

16. When air is compressed, its temperature is _____ .

17. When the fuel-air mixture reaches an excessively high temperature, _____ and _____ may take place.

18. Superchargers are classified, according to their location in the induction system of the airplane, as either _____ or _____ types.

19. When the supercharger is located between the carburetor and the cylinder intake ports, it is classified as an _____ -type supercharger.

20. An _____ -type supercharger delivers compressed air to the carburetor intake.

21. A turbocharger is an externally driven device designed to be driven by a turbine wheel which receives its power from the engine _____ .

22. The exhaust gases are usually diverted from the main exhaust stack to the turbocharger by means of a _____ .

23. The altitude above which a particular engine-supercharger combination will no longer deliver full power is called the _____ altitude.

24. The Textron Lycoming automatic turbosupercharger has three control components, which enable it to provide automatically the power that the pilot has selected for operation. These three components are the _____ controller, the _____ controller, and the _____ assembly.

25. In an air-cooled engine, thin metal fins project from the outer surfaces of the walls and heads of the engine _____ .

26. Deflector _____ fastened around the cylinders direct the flow of air to obtain the maximum cooling effect.

27. The operating temperature of the engine can be controlled by movable _____ flaps located on the engine cowling.

28. Cylinder cooling is accomplished by carrying the heat from the inside of the cylinders to the air outside the cylinders by _____ .

29. On most exhaust systems, _____ joints are provided in the system to allow for uneven expansion and contraction resulting from changes in temperature.

30. Stainless-steel shells usually referred to as _____ are placed around the mufflers to capture the heat from the mufflers and direct it to the cabin heater hoses.

Chapter 5

Name _____

Date _____

APPLICATION QUESTIONS

1. Using the figure below, identify the indicated engine induction system components.

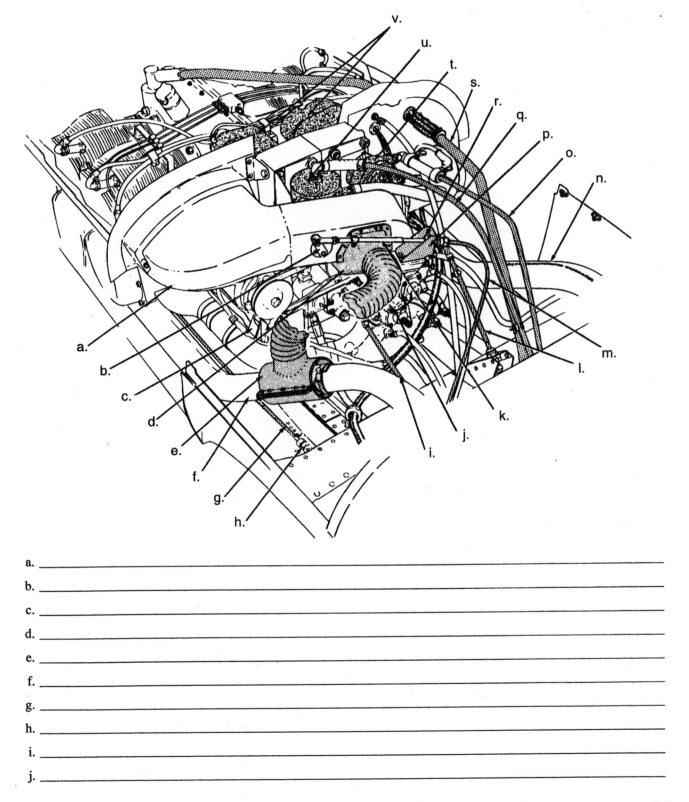

a. _____

b. _____

c. _____

d. _____

e. _____

f. _____

g. _____

h. _____

i. _____

j. _____

k. _____

l. _____

m. _____

n. _____

o. _____

p. _____

q. _____

r. _____

s. _____

t. _____

u. _____

v. _____

2. Define Boyle's Law.

_____

_____

_____

3. Define Charles' Law.

_____

_____

_____

4. What force acting in the turbocharger waste gate actuator tends to open the turbocharger waste gate?

_____

Chapter 5

REVIEW EXAM

Name _____

Date _____

1. Carburetor icing may be eliminated by which of the following methods?
   a. Alcohol spray and electrically heated induction duct
   b. Ethylene glycol spray and heated induction air
   c. Alcohol spray and heated induction air
   d. Electrically heated air intake and ethylene glycol spray

2. An increase in manifold pressure when carburetor heat is applied indicates that
   a. excessive heat is being used.
   b. ice is forming in the carburetor.
   c. the mixture is too lean.
   d. the cylinder heads are overheated.

3. As manifold pressure increases in a reciprocating engine,
   a. the volume of air in the cylinder increases.
   b. the weight of the fuel-air charge decreases.
   c. the density of air in the cylinder increases.
   d. the volume of air in the cylinder decreases.

4. If an engine is equipped with an external turbocharger and is started with the waste gate closed, the result might be
   a. some damage to cores of the turbocharger intercooler.
   b. overspeeding of the turbocharger with resultant damage to pistons and rings.
   c. serious damage because of overboost.
   d. nothing; the engine should be started with the waste gate closed.

5. The primary purpose of the diffuser vanes located in the supercharger section of a radial engine is to
   a. increase the pressure of the fuel-air charge.
   b. increase the velocity of the fuel-air charge.
   c. decrease the pressure of the fuel-air charge.
   d. increase the temperature of the fuel-air charge.

6. Which of the following would be a factor in the failure of an engine to develop full power at takeoff?
   a. Failure to install the carburetor scoop air screen
   b. Improper adjustment of carburetor heat valve control linkage
   c. Excessively rich setting on the idle mixture adjustment
   d. Failure of the economizer valve to remain closed at takeoff throttle setting

7. If the turbosupercharger waste gate is completely closed,
   a. none of the exhaust gases are directed through the turbine.
   b. the manifold pressure will be lower than normal.
   c. the turbosupercharger is in the OFF position.
   d. all the exhaust gases are directed through the turbine.

8. Boost manifold pressure is generally considered to be any manifold pressure above
   a. 14.7 inHg.
   b. 50 inHg.
   c. 40 inHg.
   d. 30 inHg.

9. What is the purpose of the density controller in a turbocharger system?
   a. To maintain constant air velocity at the carburetor venturi
   b. To limit the maximum manifold pressure that can be produced at other than full-throttle conditions
   c. To limit the maximum manifold pressure that can be produced by the turbocharger at full throttle
   d. To maintain constant air velocity at the carburetor inlet

10. What is the purpose of the rate-of-change controller in a turbocharger system?
    a. To limit the maximum manifold pressure that can be produced by the turbocharger at full-throttle conditions
    b. To limit the maximum manifold pressure that can be produced at other than full-throttle conditions
    c. To control the rate at which the turbocharger discharge pressure will increase
    d. To control the position of the waste gate after the aircraft has reached its critical altitude

11. What directly regulates the speed of a turbosupercharger?
    a. Turbine
    b. Compressor
    c. Waste gate
    d. Throttle

12. What is the purpose of a turbocharger system for a small reciprocating aircraft engine?
    a. To compress the air to hold the cabin pressure constant after the aircraft has reached its critical altitude
    b. To maintain constant air velocity in the intake manifold
    c. To compress the air to hold manifold pressure constant from sea level to the critical altitude of the engine
    d. To maintain variable air pressure to the carburetor venturi

13. The differential pressure controller in a turbocharger system
    a. reduces bootstrapping during part-throttle operation.
    b. positions the waste gate valve for maximum power.
    c. provides a constant fuel-air ratio.
    d. positions the waste gate valve to minimize exhaust back pressure.

14. What is used to drive an externally driven supercharger?
    a. Engine oil pressure
    b. A gear driven directly from the engine crankshaft
    c. Exhaust gases driving a turbine
    d. A belt driven through a pulley arrangement

15. In an airplane equipped with an alternate air system, if the main air duct air filter becomes blocked or clogged,
    a. the system will automatically allow warm, unfiltered air to be drawn into the carburetor.
    b. the flow of air to the carburetor will be slowed or cut off unless alternate air is selected.
    c. the flow of air to the carburetor will be slowed or cutoff regardless of the alternate air valve position.
    d. the system will automatically allow warm, filtered alternate air to be drawn into the carburetor.

16. On small aircraft engines, fuel vaporization may be increased by
    a. cooling the air before it enters the engine.
    b. circulating the fuel-air mixture through passages in the oil sump.
    c. heating the fuel before it enters the carburetor.
    d. routing the exhaust gases around the fuel lines.

17. A carburetor preheater is not generally used on takeoff, unless absolutely necessary, because of the
    a. resulting loss of power and possible detonation.
    b. resulting drain on the aircraft electrical system.
    c. fire hazard involved.
    d. inability of the engine to supply enough heat to make any difference.

18. What is the purpose of the augmentor used in some reciprocating engine exhaust systems?
    a. To reduce exhaust back pressure
    b. To aid in cooling the engine
    c. To assist in displacing the exhaust gases
    d. To augment the surface area of the exhaust extension

19. The purpose of an intercooler when used with a turbocharger is to
    a. cool the exhaust gases before they come in contact with the turbo drive.
    b. cool the turbocharger bearings.
    c. cool the mixture of fuel and air entering the internal turbocharger.
    d. cool the air entering the carburetor from the turbocharger.

20. Why is high nickel chromium steel used in many exhaust systems?
    a. Low expansion coefficient and high flexibility
    b. High heat conductivity and flexibility
    c. Corrosion resistance and low expansion coefficient
    d. Corrosion resistance and high heat conductivity

21. Slip joints are required in most exhaust collector systems because of the
    a. difficulty of aligning mounting bolts.
    b. necessity of installing the unit piece by piece.
    c. expansion and contraction caused by high heat and cooling.
    d. installation requirements.

22. One source commonly used for carburetor air heat is
    a. electric heating elements.
    b. cabin heater.
    c. gasoline or alcohol flame.
    d. exhaust gases.

23. What type of nuts are used to hold an exhaust system to the cylinders?
    a. Brass or special locknuts
    b. High-temperature fiber self-locking nuts
    c. Low-temperature steel self-locking nuts
    d. High-temperature aluminum self-locking nuts

24. Ball joints in reciprocating engine exhaust systems should be
    a. tight enough to prevent any movement.
    b. disassembled and have their seals replaced every engine change.
    c. secured to each exhaust extension with AN bolts, plain nuts, and lock washers.
    d. loose enough to permit some movement.

25. Augmentor tubes are part of which reciprocating engine system?
    a. Induction
    b. Oil
    c. Exhaust
    d. Fuel

Chapter 6

1. Gasoline is rated for engine fuel purposes according to its antiknock value; this value is expressed in terms of an _____ number.

2. The performance numbers of gasoline are expressed as follows: 100/130, 115/145. The first number is the _____ -performance number; the second number is the _____ -performance number.

3. Lead, in the form of _____ , is used in relatively small quantities in aviation gasoline to improve antiknock qualities.

4. The principal factors governing the grade of fuel required for an engine are the _____ and the _____ .

5. Any increase in compression ratio above that at which the fuel will burn satisfactorily under full-power conditions will cause _____ and loss of power.

6. Gravity fuel systems must be designed with the fuel tank placed far enough above the carburetor to provide such fuel pressure that the fuel flow can be _____ percent of the fuel flow required for takeoff.

7. In a pressure system, a _____ pump, usually located at the lowest point in the fuel tank, must be available for engine starting, for takeoff, for landing, and for operation at high altitudes.

8. The fuel _____ pump supplies fuel for starting the engine, and the _____ pump supplies the fuel pressure necessary for normal operation.

9. All aircraft fuel systems must be equipped with _____ and/or filters to remove dirt particles from the fuel.

10. Vapor lock in fuel systems is caused to form by the _____ atmospheric pressure of high altitude, and by _____ fuel temperature.

11. The operation of the venturi is based on _____ principle, which states that the total energy of a particle in motion is constant at all points on its path in a steady flow.

12. The pressure in the throat of the venturi tube is _____ than the pressure at either end of the tube because of the _____ velocity in the constricted portion.

13. If a fuel discharge nozzle is placed in the venturi throat of a carburetor, the effective force applied to the fuel will depend on the _____ of the air going through the venturi.

14. The ratio of fuel to air should be varied within certain limits; therefore, a _____ control system is provided for the venturi-type carburetor.

15. The mixture of fuel and air is described as _____ correct when there is just enough oxygen present in the mixture to burn the fuel completely.

16. Gasoline will burn in a cylinder if mixed with air in a ratio ranging between _____ parts of air to 1 part of fuel and _____ parts of air to 1 part of fuel (by weight).

17. A perfectly balanced fuel-air mixture has an F/A ratio of approximately 15:1, or 0.067. This is called a

_____ mixture; it is one in which all the fuel and oxygen can be combined in the burning process.

18. The ratio which shows the amount of fuel consumed by an engine in pounds per hour for each bhp developed is called

the _____ .

19. The mixture of fuel and air which will produce the greatest amount of power for a given consumption of fuel is called

the _____ mixture.

20. An excessively lean mixture may cause an engine to _____ through the induction system or to stop

completely.

21. The flame _____ in an engine cylinder is the rate at which the flame moves through the mixture of

fuel and air.

22. _____ is caused when raw fuel is permitted to flow through the intake valve into the cylinder head,

then out the exhaust valve into the exhaust stack, manifold and muffler, and heater muff.

23. A _____ is an orifice, or opening, which is carefully dimensioned to meter (measure) fuel flow

accurately in accordance with the pressure differential between the float chamber and discharge nozzle.

24. The _____ in a carburetor lifts an emulsion of air and liquid to a higher level above the liquid level

in the float chamber than would be possible with unmixed fuel.

25. The completeness of vaporization depends on the _____ of the fuel, the _____

of the air, and the _____ of atomization.

26. A _____ valve, usually a butterfly-type valve, is incorporated in the fuel-air duct to regulate the

fuel-air output.

27. The float in a carburetor is designed to control the _____ of fuel in the float chamber.

28. The _____ metering system controls the fuel feed in the upper half of the engine speed range,

which includes the speeds used for cruising and full-throttle operations.

29. An _____ valve stops the flow of fuel through an idling system on some carburetors, and this is

used for stopping the engine.

30. An _____ carburetor is one in which the air flows upward through the carburetor to the engine.

31. In many carburetors, an _____ pump is used to force an extra supply of fuel from the discharge

nozzle when the throttle is opened quickly.

32. An _____ system is essentially a valve which is closed at low engine and cruising speeds but is

opened at high speeds to provide an enriched mixture to reduce burning temperatures and prevent detonation.

33. A _____ control system can be described as a mechanism or device through which the richness of

the mixture entering the engine during flight can be controlled to a reasonable extent.

34. Mixture control systems may be classified according to their principles of operation as the _____

type, which reduces the effective suction on the metering system; the _____ type, which restricts

the flow of fuel through the metering system; and the _____ type, which allows additional air to

enter the carburetor between the main discharge nozzle and the throttle valve.

35. Some of the more complex aircraft carburetors are often equipped with a device called an _____

for automatically controlling the mixture as altitude changes.

36. The mixture control setting in the position for maximum fuel flow is the _____ position.

37. The mixture control setting which, at a given throttle setting, permits maximum engine rpm with the mixture control as far toward full rich as possible without reducing the rpm is the _____ position.

38. The mixture control setting which, at a given throttle setting, permits maximum engine rpm with the mixture control as far toward lean as possible without reducing the rpm is the _____ position.

39. A _____ carburetor takes air from above an engine and causes the air to flow down through the carburetor.

40. The process of converting a liquid to a vapor is called _____ .

41. _____ ice is most likely to form when the throttle is partially closed, such as during letdown for a landing.

42. _____ ice is formed by moisture-laden air at temperatures below freezing which strikes and freezes on elements of the induction system which are at temperatures of 32°F [0°C] or below.

43. The basic principle of the pressure injection carburetor can be explained briefly by stating that _____ is utilized to regulate the pressure of fuel to a metering system which governs the flow of fuel according to the pressure applied.

44. The four main parts of a pressure carburetor system are the _____ unit, the _____ unit, the _____ unit, and the _____ .

45. The process of using water with the F/A mixture to provide cooling for the mixture and the cylinders so that additional power can be drawn from the engine without danger of detonation is called _____ .

Chapter 6

Name _____

Date _____

APPLICATION QUESTIONS

1. Refer to the drawing of the venturi tube below and answer the following questions.

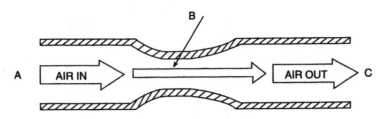

   a. At what point is the pressure the lowest: point A, point B, or point C? _____

   b. At what point is the velocity the greatest? _____

   c. At what point(s) is the pressure the highest? _____

2. Explain how lowering the pressure at some point allows the fuel to flow into the air stream.

   _____

   _____

3. Write the equation for the process which, during burning, combines isooctane with oxygen to form carbon dioxide and water.

   _____

4. Express the fuel air ratio of 12:1 as a decimal. _____

5. Express the fuel air ratio of 14:1 as a decimal. _____

6. Referring to the following chart, which engine power setting would provide the richest fuel air mixture?

   _____

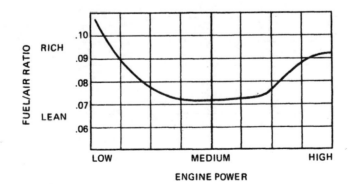

7. Identify each indicated carburetor component in the drawing below.

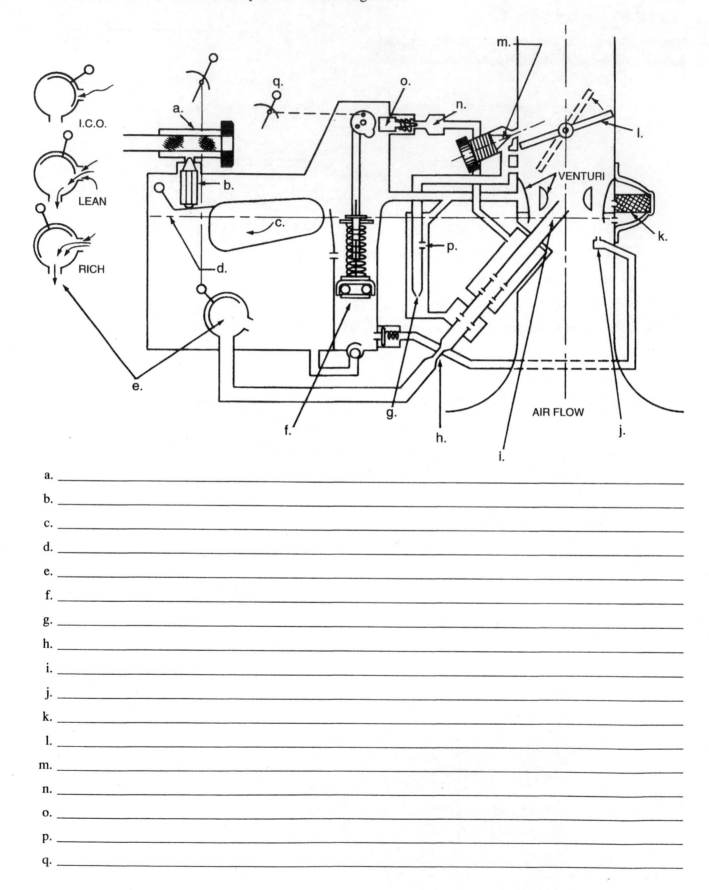

I.C.O.

LEAN

RICH

VENTURI

AIR FLOW

a. _____

b. _____

c. _____

d. _____

e. _____

f. _____

g. _____

h. _____

i. _____

j. _____

k. _____

l. _____

m. _____

n. _____

o. _____

p. _____

q. _____

8. Referring to Figure 6–54 (troubleshooting chart for float carburetors) on page 140 in the textbook, list the potential causes of the problem of an excessively lean mixture at cruising speeds.

a. _____

b. _____

c. _____

d. _____

e. _____

f. _____

g. _____

Chapter 6

Name _____

Date _____

REVIEW EXAM

1. How does injection of water or water-alcohol during high-power output increase the available power of reciprocating engines?
   a. By increasing the weight of charge
   b. By suppressing detonation
   c. By improving volumetric efficiency
   d. By increasing the burning rate of the fuel-air charge

2. A reciprocating engine automatic mixture control responds to changes in air density caused by changes in
   a. altitude or humidity.
   b. altitude only.
   c. altitude or temperature.
   d. temperature or humidity.

3. On a float-type carburetor, the purpose of the economizer valve is to
   a. economize on the amount of fuel discharged into the induction system.
   b. provide extra fuel for sudden acceleration of the engine.
   c. maintain the leanest mixture possible for cruise best power.
   d. provide a richer mixture and fuel cooling at maximum power output.

4. The fuel metering force of a conventional float-type carburetor in its normal operating range is the difference between the pressure acting on the discharge nozzle located within the venturi and the pressure
   a. acting on the fuel in the float chamber.
   b. of the fuel as it enters the carburetor.
   c. of the air as it enters the venturi (impact pressure).
   d. on the downstream or engine side of the throttle valve.

5. Which method is commonly used to adjust the level of a float in a float-type carburetor?
   a. Lengthening or shortening the float shaft
   b. Adding or removing shims under the needle valve seat
   c. Changing the angle of the float arm pivot
   d. Adding or removing float weights

6. A punctured float in a float-type carburetor will
   a. lower the fuel level and enrich the mixture.
   b. raise the fuel level and enrich the mixture.
   c. raise the fuel level and lean the mixture.
   d. lower the fuel level and lean the mixture.

7. The back-suction mixture control system operates by
   a. varying the pressure within the venturi section.
   b. altering the height of the fuel in the float chamber.
   c. varying the pressure acting on the fuel in the float chamber.
   d. changing the effective cross-sectional area of the main metering orifice (jet).

8. If an aircraft engine is equipped with a carburetor that is not compensated for altitude and temperature variations, the fuel-air mixture will become
   a. leaner as either the altitude or temperature increases.
   b. richer as the altitude increases and leaner as the temperature increases.
   c. richer as either the altitude or temperature increases.
   d. leaner as the altitude increases and richer as the temperature increases.

9. If a float-type carburetor becomes flooded, the condition is most likely to have been caused by
   a. a leaking needle valve and seat assembly.
   b. a clogged main discharge nozzle.
   c. sticking of the accelerating pump shaft.
   d. a clogged back-suction line.

10. What occurs when a back-suction-type mixture control is placed in IDLE CUTOFF?
    a. The fuel passages to the main and idle jets will be closed by a valve.
    b. The float chamber will be vented to a negative-pressure area.
    c. The fuel passage to the idle jet will be closed by a valve.
    d. The fuel passage to the main jet will be closed by a valve.

11. Which of the following best describes the function of an altitude mixture control?
    a. Regulates the richness of the fuel-air charge entering the engine
    b. Regulates the air pressure above the fuel in the float chamber
    c. Regulates the air pressure in the venturi
    d. Regulates the main airflow to the engine

12. Select the correct statement concerning the idle system of a conventional float-type carburetor.
    a. The low-pressure area created in the throat of the venturi pulls the fuel from the idle passage.
    b. Climatic conditions have very little effect on idle-mixture requirements.
    c. The low pressure between the edges of the throttle valve and the throttle body pulls the fuel from the idle passage.
    d. Airport altitude has very little effect on idle mixture requirements.

13. The economizer system of a float-type carburetor performs which of the following functions?
    a. It supplies and regulates the fuel required for all engine speeds below cruising.
    b. It supplies and regulates the fuel required for all engine speeds.
    c. It supplies and regulates the additional fuel required for all engine speeds above cruising.
    d. It regulates the fuel required for all engine speeds and all altitudes.

14. The fuel level within the float chamber of a properly adjusted float-type carburetor will be
    a. slightly higher than the discharge-nozzle outlet.
    b. unrelated to the discharge-nozzle outlet position.
    c. slightly lower than the discharge-nozzle outlet.
    d. at the same level as the discharge-nozzle outlet.

15. Select the statement which is correct in regard to a fuel level check of a float-type carburetor.
    a. Do not use leaded gasoline.
    b. Use a fuel pressure of 5 lb if the carburetor is to be used in a gravity-feed fuel system.
    c. Block off the main and idle jets to prevent a continuous flow of fuel through the jets.
    d. Do not measure the level at the edge of the float chamber.

16. What carburetor component measures the amount of air delivered to the engine?
    a. Economizer valve
    b. Automatic mixture control
    c. Cloverleaf
    d. Venturi

17. The automatic mixture control on a pressure carburetor controls the fuel-air ratio by directly controlling the
    a. air volume through the venturi.
    b. fuel pressure in chamber E.
    c. nozzle discharge orifice.
    d. air metering force.

18. In a float-type carburetor, fuel is discharged for idling speeds
    a. through the main discharge nozzle.
    b. from the idle discharge nozzle.
    c. in the venturi.
    d. through the idle discharge air bleed.

19. When air passes through the venturi of a carburetor, what three changes occur?
    a. Velocity increases, temperature increases, and pressure decreases.
    b. Velocity decreases, temperature decreases, and pressure decreases.
    c. Velocity decreases, temperature increases, and pressure increases.
    d. Velocity increases, temperature decreases, and pressure decreases.

20. Where is the throttle valve located in a float-type carburetor?
    a. Between the venturi and the discharge nozzle
    b. After the main discharge nozzle and venturi
    c. Before the venturi, but after the butterfly valve
    d. After the venturi and just before the main discharge nozzle

21. An aircraft carburetor is equipped with a mixture control in order to prevent
    a. ice from forming in the carburetor.
    b. the mixture from becoming too lean at high altitudes.
    c. the mixture from becoming too rich at high altitudes.
    d. the mixture from becoming too rich at high speeds.

22. Which of the following is not a function of the carburetor venturi?
    a. Proportioning of the air-fuel mixture
    b. Decreasing the pressure at the discharge nozzle
    c. Regulation of the idle system
    d. Limiting of the airflow at full throttle

23. What component is used to ensure fuel delivery during periods of rapid engine acceleration?
    a. Acceleration pump
    b. Standby carburetor
    c. Water injection pump
    d. Power enrichment unit

24. The device that controls the ratio of the fuel-air mixture delivered to the cylinders is called
    a. a throttle valve.
    b. a mixture control.
    c. an acceleration pump.
    d. a metering jet.

25. The device that controls the volume of the fuel-air mixture delivered to the cylinders is called
    a. an acceleration pump.
    b. a mixture control.
    c. a metering jet.
    d. a throttle valve.

26. During the operation of an aircraft engine, the pressure drop in the carburetor venturi depends primarily on the
    a. air temperature.
    b. barometric pressure.
    c. air velocity.
    d. humidity.

27. What is the purpose of the carburetor accelerating system?
    a. To supply and regulate the fuel required for engine speeds above idle
    b. To temporarily enrich the mixture when the throttle is suddenly opened
    c. To supply and regulate additional fuel required for engine speeds above cruising
    d. To temporarily derich the mixture when the throttle is suddenly closed

28. What carburetor component actually limits the desired maximum airflow to the engine at full throttle?
    a. Throttle valve
    b. Venturi
    c. Manifold intake
    d. Air diaphragm

29. On a carburetor without an automatic mixture control, as the aircraft ascends to altitude, the mixture will
    a. be enriched.
    b. be leaned.
    c. remain at the same ratio.
    d. not be affected.

30. The desired engine idle speed and mixture setting
    a. are adjusted with the engine warmed up and operating.
    b. should give minimum rpm with maximum manifold pressure.
    c. are usually adjusted in the following sequence: speed first, then mixture.
    d. are adjusted with the throttle advanced.

Chapter 7

1. A _____ system discharges the fuel into the intake port of each cylinder just ahead of the intake valve or directly into the combustion chamber of each cylinder.

Questions 2–10 apply to the Continental continous-flow fuel injection system.

2. Fuel enters the pump assembly at the _____ of the vapor separator. At this point, any vapor in the fuel is forced up to the top of the chamber, where it is drawn off by the _____ .

3. The fuel-air control unit occupies the position ordinarily used for the carburetor at the _____ inlet.

4. The unit includes three control elements, one for air in the _____ assembly and two for fuel in the _____ assembly.

5. A control lever is mounted on the mixture control valve shaft for connection to the cockpit mixture control. If the mixture control is moved toward the _____ position, the mixture control valve in the fuel control unit causes additional fuel to flow through the return line to the fuel pump.

6. The _____ valve body contains a fuel inlet, a diaphragm chamber, a valve assembly, and outlet ports for the lines to the individual fuel nozzles.

7. The fuel discharge nozzle is mounted in the _____ of the engine with its outlet directed into the intake port.

8. The Continental fuel injection system utilizes _____ (established by the engine rpm and the relief valve) and a _____ (controlled by throttle position) to meter the correct volume and pressure of fuel for all power settings.

9. The engine cannot be started without the _____ fuel pump because the engine-driven pump will not supply adequate pressure until the engine is running.

10. The engine is stopped by moving the mixture control to _____ after the engine has been idled for a short time.

Questions 11–21 apply to the Bendix RSA fuel injection system.

11. Bendix fuel injection systems are designed to meter fuel in direct ratio to the volume of _____ being consumed by the engine at a given time. This is accomplished by sensing _____ suction and _____ air pressures in the throttle body.

12. The heart of the Bendix fuel injection system is the _____ .

13. The servo valve does not meter fuel. It only controls the pressure differential across the _____ .

14. The idle mixture is correct when the engine gains approximately _____ to _____ rpm from its idle speed setting as the mixture control is placed in IDLE CUTOFF.

15. The _____ idle spring augments the force of the air diaphragm in the idle range when the air pressure differential is not sufficient to open the servo valve.

16. The AMC adjusts the F/A ratio to compensate for the decreased _____ as the aircraft climbs to altitude.

17. The two primary functions of the flow divider are

a. to ensure _____ of metered fuel to the nozzles at and just above idle, and

b. to provide isolation of each nozzle from all the others for clean engine _____ .

18. If the fuel restrictors in one or more nozzles become partially plugged, the cylinders having restricted nozzles will run _____ , and the remaining cylinders will run _____ .

19. The type of fuel nozzle in which the fuel is discharged inside the nozzle body into a chamber which is vented to either atmospheric air pressure or supercharger air pressure is called an _____ type.

20. On fuel nozzles, the letter A will be found stamped on one flat of the wrenching hexagon located _____ ° from the air-bleed hole in the nozzle body. After final installation torquing, the air bleed should be positioned _____ so that residual fuel in the line cannot drip out after engine shutdown.

21. The engine is started with the mixture control in the _____ position; as soon as the engine fires, the control is advanced to the _____ position.

Chapter 7

Name _____

Date _____

APPLICATION QUESTIONS

1. List the advantages of fuel injection over normal carburetion systems.

   a. _____

   b. _____

   c. _____

   d. _____

   e. _____

   f. _____

2. List the major components of the Continental continuous-flow fuel injection system.

   a. _____

   b. _____

   c. _____

   d. _____

3. In the Continental continuous-flow fuel injection system, what is the purpose of the orifice in the fuel injection pump?

   _____

4. With regard to fuel injection systems, where are the fuel and air first mixed before being injected into the intake port of the cylinder? _____

5. Identify the components indicated in the diagram below.

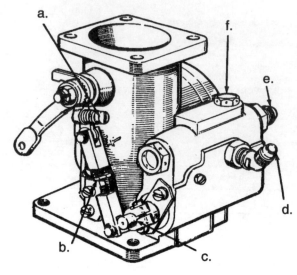

a. _____

b. _____

c. _____

d. _____

e. _____

f. _____

6. What are the names of the two diaphragms in the Bendix fuel injection system?

a. _____

b. _____

7. What two forces in the Bendix fuel injection system combine to move the air diaphragm?

a. _____

b. _____

8. Which two forces oppose each other in the regulator section of the Bendix fuel injection system?

a. _____

b. _____

9. What are the purposes of the flow divider in the Bendix fuel injection system?

a. _____

b. _____

10. Refer to Figure 7–29 (Bendix RSA fuel injection troubleshooting chart) on page 164 in the textbook, and list the probable causes of low takeoff fuel flow.

a. _____

b. _____

c. _____

d. _____

Chapter 7

Name _____

Date _____

REVIEW EXAM

1. How are discharge nozzles in a fuel injected reciprocating engine identified to indicate the flow range?
   a. By an identification letter stamped on one of the hexes of the nozzle body
   b. By drilled radial holes connecting the upper counterbore with the outside of the nozzle body
   c. By a metal identification tag attached to the nozzle body
   d. By color codes on the nozzle body

2. On a twin-engine aircraft with fuel injected reciprocating engines, one fuel flow indicator reads considerably higher than the other in all engine operating configurations. What is the probable cause of this indication?
   a. Carburetor icing
   b. One or more fuel nozzles clogged
   c. Excessive intake valve clearances
   d. Alternate air door stuck open

3. The fuel flow indication system used on most aircraft with fuel-injected opposed engines utilizes a measure of
   a. fuel flow volume.
   b. fuel pressure drop.
   c. fuel flow mass.
   d. fuel-air charge density.

4. In an aircraft equipped with a pressure-drop-type fuel flow indicating system, if one of the injector nozzles becomes restricted, this would cause
   a. a decrease in fuel flow with a decreased fuel flow indication on the gage.
   b. a decrease in fuel flow with an increased fuel flow indication on the gage.
   c. a decrease in fuel flow with no change in fuel flow indication on the gage.
   d. an increase in fuel flow with a decreased fuel flow indication on the gage.

5. An aircraft engine continuous cylinder fuel injection system normally discharges fuel into each cylinder head intake valve port during which stroke(s)?
   a. Intake
   b. Compression
   c. Intake and compression
   d. All (continuously)

6. Which statement is correct in regard to a continuous-flow fuel injection system used on some reciprocating engines?
   a. Fuel is injected directly into each cylinder.
   b. Fuel is injected at each cylinder intake port.
   c. The injection system must be timed to the engine.
   d. Two injector nozzles are used in the injector fuel system for various speeds.

7. A rotary-vane pump is best described as
   a. a positive-displacement pump.
   b. a variable-displacement pump.
   c. a boost pump.
   d. an auxiliary pump.

8. Fuel pressure produced by the engine-driven fuel pump is adjusted by the
   a. bypass valve adjusting screw.
   b. relief valve adjusting screw.
   c. main fuel strainer adjusting screw.
   d. engine-driven fuel pump adjusting screw.

9. Where would a carburetor air heater be located in a fuel injection system?
   a. Between the air intake and the cylinders
   b. At the air intake entrance
   c. None is required
   d. Between the air intake and the venturi

10. In the Bendix fuel injection system, what forces combine to move the air diaphragm?
    a. Metered fuel pressure
    b. Venturi suction and impact tube pressure
    c. Unmetered fuel pressure and pump pressure
    d. Ram air pressure and impact tube pressure

Chapter 8

1. As the piston approaches the top of its stroke within the cylinder, an _____ jumps across the points of the spark plugs and ignites the compressed F/A mixture.

2. _____ ignition is superior to battery ignition because it produces a hotter spark at high engine speeds and is a self-contained unit, not dependent on any external source of electric energy.

3. The magneto is a special type of _____ -current generator that produces electric pulsations of high voltage for purposes of ignition.

4. A _____ -tension magneto delivers current at a low voltage by means of the rotation of an armature, wound with only one coil, in the field of a permanent magnet.

5. A _____ -tension magneto delivers a high voltage and has both a primary winding and a secondary winding.

6. The inductor-rotor magneto has a _____ magnet.

7. The magneto consists of three circuits: the _____ , _____ , and _____ circuits.

8. The voltage induced in a coil of wire is proportional to the rate of change of _____ .

9. _____ law can be stated in terms of induced voltage thus: An induced voltage, whether caused by self-inductance or mutual inductance, always operates in such a direction as to oppose the source of its creation.

10. The left-hand rule states that if a wire is grasped with the left hand, and if the fingers of the left hand extend around the coil in the direction of the current, the thumb will always point in the direction of the _____ , or the _____ end of the field.

11. The typical coil assembly consists of a laminated _____ core around which is placed a primary winding and a secondary winding.

12. The _____ winding consists of a comparatively few turns of insulated copper wire, and the _____ winding consists of several thousand turns of very fine wire.

13. The breaker assembly of a magneto, also referred to as the contact breaker, consists of contact points actuated by a _____ . Its function is to open and close the circuit of the primary winding as timed to produce a buildup and collapse of the _____ .

14. The primary _____ prevents arcing between the contact points as they open by absorbing the _____ current induced in the primary coil by the collapse of the electromagnetic field established by primary current.

15. In a magneto, the number of degrees of rotation between the neutral position and the position where the contact points open is called the _____ angle.

16. The large number of _____ in the secondary winding and the very rapid change in _____ together cause a high rate of change of flux linkages, which in turn produces the high voltage in the secondary winding.

17. The distributor gear electrode (rotor) is driven at _____ engine crankshaft speed.

18. In general, the _____ of the typical aircraft magneto is a device that distributes the high-voltage current from the coil secondary terminal to the various connections of the distributor block.

19. When two magnetos fire at the same or approximately the same time through two sets of spark plugs, this is known as a _____ magneto ignition system.

20. The numbers on the distributor block show the _____ order, not the firing order of the engine.

21. To produce sparks, the rotating magnet must be turned at or above a specified rpm. This speed is known as the _____ speed of the magneto.

22. The magneto ignition switch circuit is _____ when it is turned off. This is because the purpose of the switch is to short-circuit the breaker points of the magneto and to prevent collapse of the _____ circuit required for production of a spark.

23. The ignition switch lead that connects the primary circuit and the switch is commonly referred to as the _____ .

24. When the ignition switch is in the _____ position, the switch has absolutely no effect on the primary circuit.

25. In working with the magneto system, the technician must always keep in mind that the magneto will be _____ when the P-lead is disconnected or when there is a break in the circuit leading to the ignition switch.

26. The _____ installed on the drive shaft of a magneto is designed to give the magneto a momentary high rotational speed and to provide a retarded spark for starting the engine.

27. A booster coil is a small induction coil. Its function is to provide a _____ to the spark plugs until the magneto fires properly.

28. The function of the induction vibrator is to supply interrupted low voltage (pulsating direct current) for the magneto _____ coil, which induces a sufficiently high voltage in the _____ for starting.

29. On an engine which has no propeller reduction gear, the timing mark will normally be on the _____ flange edge.

30. Timing marks, also displayed on the starter ring gear, are aligned with a small hole located on the top face of the _____ housing.

31. Timing lights are used to help determine the exact instant at which the magneto points _____ .

32. The Continental D-2000 and D-3000 magneto ignition systems were designed to provide dual ignition for aircraft engines with only _____ magneto.

33. Many magnetos that operate at high altitudes are _____ by a regulated air source from the aircraft engine.

34. The jumping of high voltage inside the distributor, called _____ , can occur, especially when the aircraft is operating at high altitudes.

35. In a radial engine, because of the mounting of the link rods on the flanges of the master rod, the travel of the pistons connected to the link rods is not uniform; therefore a _____ is utilized to obtain ignition at the correct time.

36. The _____ is the part of the ignition system in which the electric energy of the high-voltage current produced by the magneto is converted to the heat energy required to ignite the F/A mixture.

37. The spark plug provides an _____ across which the high voltage of the ignition system produces a spark to ignite the mixture.

38. An aircraft spark plug fundamentally consists of three major parts: the _____ , the _____ , and the _____ .

39. _____ -type spark plugs are designed to reduce the burning and erosion of electrodes in engines having shielded harnesses.

40. The linear distance from the shell gasket seat to the end of the shell threads, commonly referred to as the shell skirt, is called the spark plug _____ .

41. The term _____ refers to the classification of spark plugs according to their ability to transfer heat from the firing end of the spark plug to the cylinder head.

42. Fundamentally, an engine which runs hot requires a relatively _____ spark plug, whereas an engine which runs cool requires a relatively _____ spark plug.

43. If a hot spark plug is installed in an engine which runs hot, the spark plug tip will be overheated and will cause _____ .

44. If a cold spark plug is installed in an engine which runs cool, the tip of the spark plug will collect unburned carbon, causing _____ of the plug.

Chapter 8

Name _____

Date _____

APPLICATION QUESTIONS

1. List the different ways of classifying aircraft magnetos.

    a. _____ vs. _____

    b. _____ vs. _____

    c. _____ vs. _____

    d. _____ vs. _____

2. List the three circuits of a magneto.

    a. _____

    b. _____

    c. _____

3. Match the following symbols to the numbers of the correct meanings listed below.

    a. S _____

    b. D _____

    c. B _____

    d. F _____

    e. R _____

    f. L _____

    g. N _____

    (1) Double type
    (2) Flange-mounted
    (3) Bendix
    (4) Clockwise rotation as viewed from drive-shaft end
    (5) Base-mounted
    (6) Single type
    (7) Counterclockwise rotation as viewed from drive-shaft end.

4. List the basic components of the magneto in the diagram below.

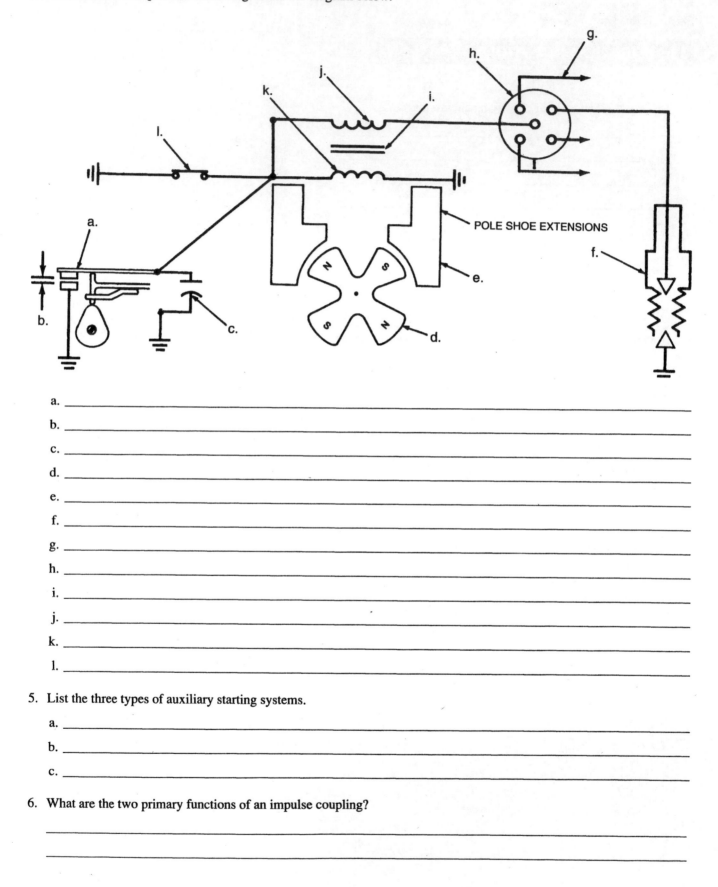

POLE SHOE EXTENSIONS

a. _____

b. _____

c. _____

d. _____

e. _____

f. _____

g. _____

h. _____

i. _____

j. _____

k. _____

l. _____

5. List the three types of auxiliary starting systems.

a. _____

b. _____

c. _____

6. What are the two primary functions of an impulse coupling?

_____

_____

7. With regard to the Continental ignition "Shower of Sparks" induction vibrator, what occurs when the retard points open?

_____

_____

_____

8. What are the two elements of magneto internal timing?

   a. _____

   b. _____

9. Define "spark plug reach."

_____

_____

_____

10. Define "spark plug heat range."

_____

_____

_____

Chapter 8

REVIEW EXAM

Name _____

Date _____

1. The E-gap angle is usually defined as the number of degrees between the neutral position of the rotating magnet and the position
   a. where the contact points close.
   b. where the contact points open.
   c. of greatest magnetic flux density.
   d. at which the secondary current is lowest.

2. The greatest density of flux lines in the magnetic circuit of a rotating magnet-type magneto occurs when the magnet is in what position?
   a. The neutral position
   b. Full alignment with the field shoe faces
   c. A certain angular displacement beyond the neutral position, referred to as the E-gap angle or position
   d. The position where the contact points open

3. Magneto breaker-point opening relative to the position of the rotating magnet and distributor rotor (internal timing) can be set most accurately
   a. after magneto-to-engine timing has been completed.
   b. during the magneto-to-engine timing operation, with subsequent in-service readjustment for wear and pitting.
   c. during assembly of the magneto before installation on the engine.
   d. by setting the points roughly at the required clearance before installing the magneto and then making the fine breaker-point adjustment after installation to compensate for wear in the magneto drive train.

4. What is the purpose of a safety gap in some magnetos?
   a. To discharge the secondary coil's voltage if an open occurs in the secondary circuit
   b. To ground the magneto when the ignition switch is off
   c. To keep the magneto from delivering a spark until it reaches its coming-on speed
   d. To prevent flashover in the distributor

5. When a magneto is being timed internally, the alignment of the timing marks indicates that
   a. the breaker points are just closing.
   b. the magnets are in the neutral position.
   c. the magnets are in the E-gap position.
   d. the breaker points are open to their widest gap.

6. When a magneto is being timed internally, the breaker points begin to open when the rotating magnet is
   a. in the neutral position.
   b. fully aligned with the pole shoes.
   c. a few degrees past full alignment with the pole shoes.
   d. a few degrees past the neutral position.

7. What is the electrical location of the primary condenser in a high-tension magneto?
   a. Across the ignition switch
   b. Across the breaker points
   c. In series with the breaker points
   d. Between the ignition switch and the breaker points

8. In a high-tension ignition system, the current in the magneto secondary winding is
   a. conducted from the primary winding via the discharge of the condenser.
   b. conducted from the primary by the counter emf developed across the condenser.
   c. induced when the primary circuit is interrupted.
   d. induced when the primary circuit discharges via the breaker points.

9. When a "Shower of Sparks" ignition system is activated at an engine start, a spark plug fires
   a. as soon as the retard breaker points close.
   b. as soon as the advance breaker points open.
   c. only while both the retard and advance breaker points are closed.
   d. only while both the retard and advance breaker points are open.

10. Magneto pole shoes are generally made of
    a. laminations of high-grade soft iron.
    b. laminations of high-grade alnico.
    c. strips of extremely hard steel.
    d. pieces of high-carbon iron.

11. Capacitance afterfiring in most modern spark plugs is reduced by the use of
    a. massive electrodes.
    b. fine wire electrodes.
    c. a built-in resistor in each plug.
    d. aluminum oxide insulation.

12. What component(s) make(s) up the magnetic system of a magneto?
    a. Pole shoes, pole shoe extensions, and primary coil
    b. Primary and secondary coils
    c. Rotating magnet, pole shoes, pole shoe extensions, and coil core
    d. Rotating magnet

13. In an aircraft ignition system, one of the functions of the condenser is to
    a. regulate the flow of current between the primary and secondary coils.
    b. facilitate a more rapid collapse of the charge in the primary coil.
    c. stop the flow of magnetic lines of force when the points open.
    d. act as a safety gap for the secondary coil.

14. As an aircraft engine's speed is increased, the voltage induced in the primary coil of the magneto
    a. remains constant.
    b. increases.
    c. varies with the setting of the voltage regulator.
    d. decreases.

15. During internal timing of a magneto, the breaker points begin to open when
    a. the piston has just passed TDC at the end of the compression stroke.
    b. the resultant flux flow is zero.
    c. the magnet poles are a few degrees beyond the neutral position.
    d. the magnet poles are fully aligned with the pole shoes.

16. A defective primary condenser in a magneto is indicated by
    a. broken breaker points.
    b. a fine-grained frosted appearance of the breaker points
    c. burned and pitted breaker points.
    d. weak spark.

17. A magneto ignition switch is connected
    a. in series with the breaker points.
    b. in series with both the breaker points and the primary condenser.
    c. parallel to the breaker points.
    d. in series with the primary condenser and parallel to the breaker points.

18. The spark is produced in a magneto ignition system when the breaker points are
    a. beginning to close.
    b. fully open.
    c. beginning to open.
    d. fully closed.

19. Shielding is used on spark plug and ignition wires to
    a. prevent leakage of current which results in a weak spark.
    b. protect the wires from short circuits as a result of chafing and rubbing.
    c. protect the wires from oil and grease.
    d. prevent interference with radio reception.

20. What is the purpose of using an impulse coupling with a magneto?
    a. To absorb impulse vibrations between the magneto and the engine
    b. To compensate for backlash in the magneto and the engine gears
    c. To produce a momentary high rotational speed of the magneto
    d. To prevent the magneto speed from fluctuating at high engine speeds

21. Failure of an engine to cease firing after the magneto switch has been turned off is an indication of
    a. a grounded magneto lead.
    b. an open in the low-tension lead to ground.
    c. a grounded condenser.
    d. a grounded magneto switch.

22. Alignment of the marks provided for internal timing of a magneto indicates that
    a. the breaker points are just beginning to close for the No. 1 cylinder.
    b. the magneto is in the E-gap position.
    c. the No. 1 cylinder is at TDC of the compression stroke.
    d. the distributor gear is correctly aligned with the rotor shaft.

23. What is the difference between a low-tension and a high-tension ignition system?
    a. A low-tension system produces relatively low voltage at the spark plug compared with a high-tension system.
    b. A low-tension system does not require high-voltage leads, but a high-tension system requires all leads to transmit high voltage.
    c. A high-tension system is designed for high-altitude aircraft, whereas a low-tension system is designed for low- to medium-altitude aircraft.
    d. A low-tension system uses a transformer coil near the spark plugs to boost voltage, whereas a high-tension system has constant voltage from the magneto to the spark plugs.

24. The amount of voltage generated in any magneto secondary coil is determined by the number of windings and by
    a. the rate of buildup of the magnetic field around the primary coil.
    b. the rate of collapse of the magnetic field around the primary coil.
    c. the amount of charge stored by the capacitor.
    d. the amount of charge released by the capacitor.

25. Magneto breaker points must be timed to open when
    a. the rotating magnet is positioned a few degrees before neutral.
    b. the greatest magnetic field stress exists in the magnetic circuit.
    c. the least magnetic field stress exists in the magnetic circuit.
    d. the rotating magnet is in the full register position.

26. In a low-tension ignition system, each spark plug requires an individual
    a. condenser.
    b. cam assembly.
    c. breaker assembly.
    d. secondary coil.

27. The electrical circuit from the spark plug back to the magneto is completed by
    a. grounding through the engine structure to the magneto.
    b. grounding through the fuselage to earth.
    c. grounding through spark plug lead shielding to the magneto.
    d. a ground wire through the cockpit switch.

28. Which of the following will cause the center electrode insulator of ceramic spark plugs to fracture and/or break?
    a. Improper timing
    b. Electrical erosion
    c. Improper gapping procedures
    d. Excessive magneto voltage

29. When the ignition switch of a single (reciprocating) engine aircraft is turned to the OFF position,
    a. the primary circuits of both magnetos are grounded.
    b. the secondary circuits of both magnetos are opened.
    c. all circuits are automatically opened.
    d. the high-tension lead from the battery is grounded.

30. A spark plug's heat range is the result of its specific design, and therefore of
    a. the area of the plug exposed to the cooling airstream.
    b. its ability to transfer heat from the firing end to the cylinder head.
    c. the area of the plug terminal.
    d. the heat intensity of the spark.

31. The term "reach," as applied to spark plug design and/or type, indicates
    a. the length of the center electrode insulation exposed to the flame of combustion.
    b. the linear distance from the shell gasket seat to the end of the shell skirt.
    c. the length of the center electrode exposed to the flame of combustion.
    d. the length of the shielded barrel.

32. The numbers appearing on the ignition distributor block indicate
    a. the sparking order of the distributor.
    b. the relation between distributor terminal numbers and cylinder numbers.
    c. the ratio of the distributor rotor speed to the crankshaft speed.
    d. the firing order of the engine.

33. Compensated timing provides for the firing of the cylinders
    a. at the position of crankshaft travel that provides the balance between the inertia of the reciprocating mass and the force that results from compressing the fuel-air charge.
    b. at the piston position which produces peak compression regardless of the degree of crankshaft travel required to obtain that position.
    c. an equal number of degrees of crankshaft travel apart regardless of variations in piston position caused by articulation of the connecting rod assembly.
    d. in relationship to piston position regardless of variations in crankshaft travel required to obtain that position.

34. Hot spark plugs are generally used in aircraft power-plants
    a. with comparatively high compression or high operating temperatures.
    b. with comparatively low operating temperatures.
    c. which are loosely baffled.
    d. which produce high power per cubic inch of displacement.

35. If a spark plug lead becomes grounded,
    a. the magneto secondary winding will become overloaded and break down.
    b. the magneto will not be affected.
    c. the distributor rotor finger will discharge to the next closest electrode within the distributor.
    d. the condenser will break down.

36. Which of the following statements regarding magneto switch circuits is false?
    a. In the BOTH position, the right and left magneto circuits are grounded.
    b. In the OFF position, neither the right nor the left magneto circuit is open.
    c. In the RIGHT position, the right magneto circuit is open and the left magneto circuit is grounded.
    d. In the LEFT position, the left magneto circuit is open and the right magneto circuit is grounded.

37. A spark plug is fouled when
    a. its gap is too small.
    b. its magneto wire is not connected.
    c. it causes preignition.
    d. its spark grounds without jumping electrodes.

38. Which of the following would be cause for rejection of a spark plug?
    a. Carbon fouling of the electrode and insulator
    b. Cracked insulator tip
    c. Light gray coloration of the center electrode
    d. Lead fouling of the electrode and insulator

39. What will be the result of using an excessively hot spark plug?
    a. Failure of the engine
    b. Fouling of the plug
    c. Preignition
    d. Burning of the condenser

40. If new breaker points are installed in a magneto on an engine, it will be necessary to time
    a. the magneto internally and the magneto to the engine.
    b. the breaker points to the No. 1 cylinder.
    c. the magneto drive to the engine.
    d. the distributor gear to the magneto drive

Chapter 9

STUDY QUESTIONS

1. If an engine fire occurs while the engine is being started, the fuel shutoff lever should be moved to the _____ position.

2. If an engine fire persists, _____ can be discharged into the inlet duct while the engine is being cranked.

3. Ground support personnel who are in the vicinity of aircraft that are being run up need to wear proper _____ and _____ protection.

Questions 4–7 apply to starting of float carburetors.

4. The throttle should be opened approximately _____ in.

5. If the engine is equipped with a constant-speed propeller, the propeller control should be set at the _____ position.

6. The carburetor heat lever should be set at the _____ position.

7. The mixture lever should be set at the _____ position.

Questions 8–10 apply to starting of engines equipped with Bendix fuel injection systems.

8. The mixture control should initially be in the _____ position.

9. Priming of the engine is begun by adjusting the throttle to _____ inch open. Then the mixture control is moved to _____ until the fuel flow gage reads 4 to 6 gal/h [15.14 to 22.7 L/h] and is immediately returned to _____ .

10. As soon as the engine starts, the mixture control is moved to _____ .

11. When an engine starts, an oil pressure indication should register within _____ s in normal weather and _____ s in cold weather. If no indication appears, the engine should be _____ and the problem investigated.

12. Before any attempt is made to start a large reciprocating engine, the engine should be rotated several complete revolutions to eliminate the possibility of _____ , which is caused by oil in the lower cylinders.

13. The permissible rpm drop during the magneto test varies, but it is usually between _____ and _____ rpm.

14. When the magnetos are checked on an airplane having a constant-speed or controllable-pitch propeller, it is essential that the propeller be in the full _____ position; otherwise, a true indication of rpm drop may not be obtained.

15. During the pretakeoff propeller check, the propeller is _____ so as to circulate the cold oil from the propeller hub and to allow warmer oil to enter the hub.

16. Continued climb at maximum power can produce excessive _____ and detonation.

17. Power should not be reduced suddenly when the CHT is high. The sudden cooling which occurs when power is reduced sharply will often cause the _____ to crack.

18. During operation of an airplane with a constant-speed propeller, _____ should always be reduced with the throttle before the _____ is reduced with the propeller control. Conversely, the _____ should always be increased with the propeller control before _____ is increased.

19. During a prolonged glide with power low (throttle near closed position), one should _____ occasionally to prevent spark plug fouling.

20. The engine should be operated with the mixture control in a LEAN position only during _____ flight.

21. If there is any possibility of ice forming in the carburetor while power is reduced for a letdown preparatory to landing, it is necessary to place the carburetor heat control in the _____ position.

22. An engine should be stopped by placing the mixture control in the _____ position.

23. Many engines that were formerly operated on 80/87-octane avgas are now being run on 100LL avgas. This presents the problem of _____ , because 100LL avgas contains four times the TEL (tetraethyl-lead) of 80/87-octane avgas.

24. Proper draining of the _____ sump is very important during the preflight check. Sufficient fuel should be drawn off into a transparent container to see if the fuel is free of _____ and _____ .

25. _____ of an engine consists of forcing heated air into the engine area to heat the engine, lubricants, and accessories.

26. During an inspection, a checklist must be used that meets the scope and detail of FAR _____ , Appendix _____ .

27. The spin-on filter is inspected for evidence of _____ particles that could indicate internal engine damage.

28. The purpose of testing cylinder _____ is to determine the internal condition of the combustion chamber by ascertaining if any appreciable leakage is occurring.

29. The two basic types of compression testers currently in use are the _____ tester and the _____ tester.

30. During a differential-pressure compression test, a loss in excess of _____ % of input air pressure is cause to suspect the cylinder of being defective.

31. If air is leaking from the _____ , the technician will hear air exiting from the exhaust stacks or carburetor inlet.

32. Exhaust manifold and stack fatigue failures usually occur at _____ or _____ joints.

33. Lead pencils must not be used to mark _____ system parts. At high temperatures, the softened metal will likely be subject to the development of _____ in the marked areas.

34. The shock mounts on a _____ engine mount point toward the center of gravity of the engine.

35. _____ is the step-by-step procedure used to determine the cause of a given fault and then selection of the best and quickest solution.

36. If blue oil smoke is emitted from the engine breather and exhaust, most likely the _____ are worn, so that blowby occurs.

37. _____ occurs when the flame from the combustion chamber burns back into the intake manifold and ignites the F/A mixture before the mixture enters the engine.

38. _____ is the burning of F/A mixture in the exhaust manifold after the mixture has passed through the exhaust valve.

Chapter 9

Name _____

Date _____

APPLICATION QUESTIONS

1. List the steps of the starting procedure for an aircraft engine with a float-type carburetor.

    a. _____

    b. _____

    c. _____

    d. _____

    e. _____

    f. _____

    g. _____

    h. _____

    i. _____

2. The conditions that must be checked during the operation of the engine are:

    a. _____

    b. _____

    c. _____

    d. _____

    e. _____

    f. _____

    g. _____

    h. _____

3. What is the advantage of leaning the mixture during cruise operation?

    _____

    _____

4. What is the air pressure used on a pressure regulator during a differential-compression test?

    _____

5. How much of a pressure loss in the cylinder during a differential-compression test would be a basis for suspecting the cylinder of being defective? _____

6. List three different types of air filters.

    a. _____

    b. _____

    c. _____

7. List the steps in troubleshooting.

a. _____

b. _____

c. _____

d. _____

e. _____

f. _____

8. Refer to Figures 9–15 and 9–16 on pages 232 and 233 in the textbook, and list the probable causes of the following combination of engine indications: engine will not start, engine cranking, all circuit breakers and switches in correct position.

a. _____

b. _____

c. _____

d. _____

Chapter 9

REVIEW EXAM

1. Which of the following is required by FAR part 43 when performing a 100-hour inspection on a reciprocating engine?
   a. Magneto timing check
   b. Cylinder compression check
   c. Valve timing check
   d. Crankshaft runout check

2. As the pressure is applied during a reciprocating engine compression check using a differential-pressure tester, what does a movement of the propeller in the direction of the engine rotation indicate?
   a. The piston is positioned ahead of top dead center.
   b. The piston is on the compression stroke.
   c. The piston is on the intake stroke.
   d. The piston is positioned past top dead center.

3. During routine inspection of a reciprocating engine, a deposit of small, bright, metallic particles which do not cling to the magnetic drain plug is discovered in the oil sump and on the surface of the oil filter. This condition
   a. may be a result of abnormal plain-type bearing wear and is cause for further investigation.
   b. indicates accessory section gear wear and is cause for removal and/or overhaul.
   c. is probably a result of ring and cylinder wall wear and is cause for engine removal and/or overhaul.
   d. is normal in engines utilizing plain-type bearings and aluminum pistons and is not cause for alarm.

4. Before an attempt is made to start a radial engine that has been shut down for more than 30 minutes,
   a. the fuel selector valve should be placed in the OFF position.
   b. the propeller should be pulled through by hand in the opposite direction of normal rotation to check for liquid lock.
   c. the ignition switch should be turned on before the starter is energized.
   d. the propeller should be turned three to four revolutions in the normal direction of rotation to check for liquid lock.

5. An engine misses with the magneto switch at either the right or the left position. The quickest method for locating the trouble is to
   a. check for cold cylinders to isolate the trouble.
   b. perform a compression check.
   c. check for a weak breaker spring in the magneto.
   d. check each spark plug.

6. By use of a differential-pressure compression tester, it is determined that the No. 3 cylinder of a nine-cylinder radial engine will not hold pressure after the crankshaft has been rotated 260° from top dead center on the compression stroke of the No. 1 cylinder. How can this indication usually be interpreted?
   a. Badly worn or damaged piston rings.
   b. A normal indication.
   c. Exhaust valve blowby.
   d. A damaged exhaust valve or insufficient exhaust valve clearance.

7. What is the basic operational sequence for reducing the power output of an engine equipped with a constant-speed propeller?
   a. Reduce the rpm, then the manifold pressure.
   b. Reduce the rpm, then adjust the propeller control.
   c. Reduce the manifold pressure, then retard the throttle to obtain the correct rpm.
   d. Reduce the manifold pressure, then the rpm.

8. Which of the following would most likely cause a reciprocating engine to backfire through the induction system at low-rpm operation?
   a. Idle speed too low
   b. Idle mixture too rich
   c. Clogged derichment valve
   d. Lean mixture

9. When will small induction system air leaks have the most noticeable effect on engine operation?
   a. At medium to high cruise power settings
   b. At high rpm
   c. At maximum continuous and takeoff power settings
   d. At low rpm

10. What could cause excessive pressure buildup in the crankcase of a reciprocating engine?
    a. Plugged crankcase breather
    b. Oil pump pressure adjusted too high
    c. An excessive quantity of oil
    d. Worn oil scavenge pump

11. If air is heard coming from the crankcase breather or oil filler during a differential compression check, what is this an indication of?
    a. Exhaust valve leakage
    b. Intake valve leakage
    c. Piston ring leakage
    d. The piston is not on the compression stroke

12. One cause of afterfiring in an aircraft engine is
    a. early timing.
    b. sticking intake valves.
    c. an excessively lean mixture.
    d. an excessively rich mixture.

13. Which of the following component inspections is to be accomplished during a 100-hour inspection?
    a. Check internal timing of magneto.
    b. Check cylinder compression.
    c. Check float level.
    d. Check valve timing.

14. Which of the following, obtained during a magneto check at 1700 rpm, indicates a short (grounded) circuit between the right magneto primary and the ignition switch?
    a. BOTH—1700 rpm, R—1625 rpm, L—1700 rpm, OFF—1625 rpm
    b. BOTH—1700 rpm, R—0 rpm, L—1700 rpm, OFF—0 rpm
    c. BOTH—1700 rpm, R—1625 rpm, L—1675 rpm, OFF—1625 rpm
    d. BOTH—1700 rpm, R—0 rpm, L—1675 rpm, OFF—0 rpm

15. When performing a magneto ground check on an engine, correct operation is indicated by
    a. a decrease in manifold pressure.
    b. an increase in rpm.
    c. no drop in rpm.
    d. a slight drop in rpm.

16. Defective spark plugs will cause
    a. intermittent missing of the engine at high speeds only.
    b. intermittent missing of the engine at low speeds only.
    c. failure of the magneto.
    d. intermittent missing of the engine at all speeds.

17. On an aircraft that utilizes an exhaust heat exchanger as a source of cabin heat, how should the exhaust system be inspected?
    a. X-rayed to detect any cracks
    b. Tested by use of an exhaust gas analyzer
    c. Hydrostatically tested
    d. With the heater air shroud removed

18. All of the following are recommended markers for reciprocating engine exhaust systems except
    a. India ink.
    b. chalk.
    c. lead pencil.
    d. Prussian blue.

19. What could be a result of undetected exhaust system leaks in a reciprocating engine powered airplane?
    a. Pilot incapacitation resulting from carbon monoxide entering the cabin
    b. A rough-running engine
    c. Nonattainment of desired power settings
    d. Excessive engine operating temperatures

20. By what indications may reciprocating engine exhaust system leaks be detected?
    a. An exhaust trail aft of the tailpipe on the airplane exterior
    b. Low cylinder-head temperature indication
    c. Fluctuating manifold pressure indication
    d. Signs of exhaust soot inside cowling and on adjacent components

Chapter 10

STUDY QUESTIONS

1. The recommended overhaul time is determined by the _____ for each model of engine based on experience.

2. An overhaul performed on the engine which reconditions only the cylinders, pistons, and valve operating mechanism is called a _____ overhaul.

3. The actual time between overhauls (TBO) for a given engine is determined largely by the manner of its _____ .

4. An _____ engine, according to the FAA, is one that has been disassembled, cleaned, inspected, repaired as necessary, reassembled, and tested according to the manufacturer's instructions and specifications.

5. A _____ engine must meet the same limits and tolerances as specified by the engine manufacturer.

6. A rebuilt engine does not have to carry the previous operating history when it is returned to service. It can be said that the engine has been granted _____ .

7. An aircraft engine may be labeled as rebuilt only by the _____ or an agency approved by the _____ .

8. A major overhaul can be performed or supervised by the powerplant mechanic and does not require FAA form 337 unless the engine is equipped with an _____ supercharger or has a _____ reduction system with other than spur-type gears.

9. Every engine overhaul must be accomplished in accordance with the instructions given in the manufacturer's _____ manual.

10. To provide overhaul services for certificated aircraft engines, an overhaul agency should be an FAA _____ with ratings to cover all types of overhaul work performed.

11. The purpose of the _____ inspection is to determine the general condition of the engine when it is received and to provide an inventory of the engine and all its accessories and associated parts.

12. The FAA Type Certificate Data Sheet must be reviewed to ensure that the engine _____ to its type certification.

13. From time to time, special _____ are issued by an engine manufacturer to require alterations or parts replacements designed to improve the performance and reliability of the engine.

14. The FAA issues _____ pertaining to aircraft and engines whenever it appears that certain changes should be made to correct discrepancies or to improve the reliability of the unit.

15. The inspection record should show the dimensions of each part measured and all fits and clearances. These measurements are compared with the manufacturer's _____ .

16. During _____ , the operator should identify and mark all parts.

17. Visual inspection is accomplished by direct examination and with the use of a _____ .

18. Roughness in an area where material has been eroded by foreign material being rubbed between moving surfaces is called _____ .

19. The separation of metal or other material, usually caused by various types of stress, including fatigue stress caused by repeated loads, is called a _____ .

20. The surface erosion caused by very slight movement between two surfaces which are tightly pressed together is called

_____ .

21. The tearing away of metal by a hard object being moved along a softer surface under heavy force is called _____ .

22. Chemical combination of a metal with atmospheric oxygen results in _____ .

23. Deep scratches or grooves caused by hard particles between moving surfaces are called _____ .

24. In general, two types of cleaning are required when an engine is overhauled: _____ , which is the removal of oil, soft types of dirt, and soft carbon (sludge); and _____ , which is the removal of hard carbon deposits.

25. The function of the _____ inspection is to determine the structural integrity of each part.

26. Magnetic particle testing is a nondestructive method for locating surface and subsurface discontinuities (cracks or defects) in _____ materials.

27. Parts are magnetized by passing a strong _____ through or around them.

29. The ease with which a magnetic field can be set up in a magnetic circuit is called _____ .

29. Engine parts made of aluminum alloy such as crankcase halves and accessory cases are typically inspected with

_____ .

30. _____ inspection utilizes high-frequency sound waves to reveal flaws in metal parts.

31. An _____ tester applies high-frequency electromagnetic waves to the metal, and these waves generate eddy currents inside the metal.

32. _____ inspections are employed to determine the degree of wear for parts of the engine where moving surfaces are in contact with other surfaces.

33. Cylinder barrels are generally measured with a cylinder _____ .

34. The dimensions of small gaps, such as the clearances between piston rings and ring lands, are measured with a _____ gage.

35. Checking the runout or out-of-roundness of rotating parts, such as crankshafts and camshafts, is accomplished with a

_____ .

36. Valve seats can usually be repaired by _____ with specially designed seat grinding equipment.

37. The use of a narrow contact surface between valves and valve seats to obtain a more positive seal is called an

_____ .

38. A thin edge on a valve is called a feather edge and can lead to _____ .

39. After valves and seats are ground, they are _____ to provide a gastight and liquid-tight seal.

40. When the cylinders of an engine have been chromium plated, the piston rings used in these cylinders must be made of unplated _____ or _____ .

41. A cylinder _____ machine is used for final finishing of the cylinder walls.

42. A chocked cylinder barrel is usually designed with a slightly _____ dimension at the top than at the skirt.

43. When a threaded hole has been damaged or oversized beyond accepted limits, it can be repaired by retapping and installing a _____ insert.

44. Manufacturers generally agree that the following parts should be replaced at overhaul:

a. _____

b. _____

c. _____

d. _____

e. _____

f. _____

g. _____

h. _____

45. One of the most important factors that a technician must consider in the assembly of an engine or other parts of an aircraft is the _____ applied in tightening of nuts and bolts.

46. Before an engine is actually started for the first time, it should be _____ to remove trapped air in oil passages and lines and to ensure that all bearing surfaces are lubricated.

47. If an engine is to be stored for a time after having been run in, it should be preserved against _____ .

Chapter 10

Name _____

Date _____

APPLICATION QUESTIONS

1. List the basic steps in the overhaul process.

   a. _____

   b. _____

   c. _____

   d. _____

   e. _____

   f. _____

   g. _____

   h. _____

   i. _____

   j. _____

   k. _____

2. Define the term "chafing."

   _____

   _____

   _____

3. Define the term "fretting."

   _____

   _____

   _____

4. Define the term "galling."

   _____

   _____

   _____

5. Define the term "scoring."

   _____

   _____

   _____

6. Because agents used for stripping can be hazardous to parts and to personnel performing this operation, list the precautions which should be observed.

a. _____

b. _____

c. _____

d. _____

e. _____

f. _____

7. Explain circular magnetization.

_____

_____

_____

8. Explain longitudinal magnetization.

_____

_____

_____

9. Why are dimensional inspections employed during the overhaul process?

_____

_____

_____

10. What type of machine is used to reface valves? _____

11. When a stud is replaced, the replacement stud should be _____ size larger than the stud removed.

12. What is the color code of a 0.009-in oversized stud? _____

Questions 13 and 14 refer to the use of a torque wrench in conjunction with an extension on the torque wrench.

13. If an actual torgue of 100 in•lb is to be applied to a bolt, using an 8-in-long torque wrench with a 4-in-long extension, what should be the reading on the torque wrench? _____

14. If an actual torque of 120 in•lb is to be applied to a bolt, using a 12-in-long torque wrench with a 6-in-long extension, what should be the reading on the torque wrench? _____

15. During the break-in or engine test period, during run No. 5, at what rpm should the engine be run, and for how long should it be run?

_____

Chapter 10

REVIEW EXAM

1. If the crankshaft runout readings on the dial indicator are +0.002 in and –0.003 in, the runout is
   a. 0.005 in.
   b. 0.001 in.
   c. +0.001 in.
   d. –0.001 in.

2. Consider the following statements:
   (1) Only cast-iron piston rings can be used in nitrided or chromium-plated cylinders.
   (2) Chromium-plated rings may be used in plain steel cylinders.
   Of these two statements,
   a. only No. 1 is true.
   b. only No. 2 is true.
   c. neither No. 1 nor No. 2 is true.
   d. both No. 1 and No. 2 are true.

3. How is proper end-gap clearance on new piston rings ensured during the major overhaul of an engine?
   a. By using a go and no-go gage
   b. By using rings specified by the engine manufacturer
   c. By placing the rings in the cylinder and measuring the end gap with a feeler gage
   d. By grinding the rings on an emery wheel

4. On which part of the cylinder walls of a normally operating engine will the greatest amount of wear occur?
   a. On the lower walls of the cylinders that are installed horizontally
   b. Near the center of the cylinder where piston velocity is the greatest
   c. Near the top of the cylinder
   d. Near the bottom of the cylinder

5. During overhaul, reciprocating engine intake and exhaust valves are checked for stretch
   a. with a suitable outside micrometer caliper.
   b. with a contour gage.
   c. with a suitable vernier caliper.
   d. by placing the valve on a surface plate and measuring its length with a vernier height gage.

6. Crankshaft runout is checked
   a. after each flight and after a 30-day layoff.
   b. during engine overhaul and in case of sudden stoppage of the engine.
   c. during engine overhaul and anytime it is convenient.
   d. if the propeller is too noisy and vibrates.

7. If an engine cylinder is to be removed, at what position in the cylinder should the piston be?
   a. Bottom dead center
   b. Top dead center
   c. Halfway between top and bottom dead center
   d. Any convenient position

8. Which of the following engine servicing operations generally requires engine pre-oiling prior to starting the engine?
   a. Oil filter change
   b. Engine oil change
   c. Engine installation
   d. Replacement of oil lines

9. When can it be concluded that a reciprocating engine with a dry sump has been pre-oiled sufficiently?
   a. When oil appears on the cylinder interior walls
   b. When the engine oil pressure gage indicates normal oil pressure
   c. When oil flows from the engine return line or indicator port
   d. When the quantity of oil specified by the manufacturer has been pumped into the engine

10. Straightening of nitrided crankshafts is
    a. recommended.
    b. not recommended.
    c. approved by repair stations.
    d. approved by the manufacturer.

11. A severe condition of chafing or fretting, in which a transfer of metal from one part to another occurs, is called
    a. gouging.
    b. burning.
    c. erosion.
    d. galling.

12. Which of the following can inspect and approve an engine for return to service following major repair?
    a. Certificated mechanic with airframe and powerplant ratings
    b. Certificated mechanic with a powerplant rating
    c. Certificated mechanic with inspection authorization
    d. Designated Mechanic Examiner

13. Which of the following contains approved data for performing a major repair on an aircraft engine?
    a. Engine Type Certificate Data Sheets
    b. Supplemental Type Certificates
    c. Technical Standard Orders
    d. Manufacturer's Maintenance Manual when FAA approved

14. What maintenance record(s) is (are) required following a major repair of an aircraft engine?
    a. Entries in the airplane flight manual and aircraft logbook
    b. Entries in engine maintenance records and a list of discrepancies for the FAA
    c. Entries in the engine maintenance record and FAA Form 337
    d. Entry in logbook

15. Which of the following defects would likely cause a hot spot on a reciprocating engine cylinder?
    a. Too much cooling fin area broken off
    b. A cracked cylinder baffle
    c. A cracked cylinder baffle blast tube
    d. Cowling air seal leakage

Chapter 11

STUDY QUESTIONS

1. A _____ engine is a mechanical device which produces forward thrust by forcing the movement of a mass of gases rearward.

2. The amount of force or thrust produced depends on the _____ of the air moved through the engine and the extent to which this air can be _____ and ejected.

3. The amount of acceleration of an object is _____ to the force applied.

4. Acceleration = _____ / _____ .

5. The _____ jet engine is the simplest of the jet engines in that it contains no moving parts.

6. A gas-turbine engine has three major sections: an _____ , a _____ , and a _____ .

7. Aircraft turbine engines can generally be classified into four types: _____ , _____ , _____ , and _____ .

8. A turbojet engine is a type of gas-turbine engine which produces thrust through the ejection of _____ from the exhaust section of the engine.

9. The _____ engine accelerates a smaller volume of air than the turboprop engine but a larger volume than the turbojet engine.

10. Turbofan engines may be _____ -bypass or _____ -bypass engines.

11. A _____ -bypass engine does not bypass as much air around the core as a _____ -bypass engine.

12. On some front-fan engines, the bypass airstream is ducted overboard either directly behind the fan through short ducts or at the rear of the engine through longer ducts, thus the term _____ .

13. A _____ engine is nothing more than a gas-turbine or turbojet engine with a reduction gearbox mounted in the front or forward end to drive a standard airplane propeller.

14. A _____ engine is a gas-turbine engine which delivers shaft horsepower through an output shaft.

15. Acceleration may be defined as a change in _____ .

16. Mass is a basic property of matter, whereas _____ is the effect of gravity on a mass.

17. _____ law states that the volume of a confined body of gas varies inversely as its absolute pressure, the temperature remaining constant.

18. _____ law states that the volume of a gas varies in direct proportion to the absolute temperature.

19. _____ is a reaction force which is measured in pounds.

20. _____ is the mass per unit of volume or the number of molecules per unit of volume.

21. As the air temperature increases, thrust tends to _____ .

22. As density goes up, the weight of air goes up and consequently the thrust goes _____ .

23. At low engine speeds, the turbojet thrust increase is _____ , even for a large increase in engine speed.

24. The effect of humidity on turbine-engine output is almost _____ .

25. About 10 to 15% additional thrust can be gained by injecting _____ into the engine, either at the compressor air inlet or at some other point in the engine.

26. Water injection does two things directly: it _____ the air mass and maintains the same _____ by adding molecules to the mass flow.

27. The efficiency of any engine can be described as the _____ divided by the _____ .

28. One of the main measures of turbine-engine efficiency is the amount of thrust produced or generated, divided by the fuel consumption. This is called _____ .

29. Propulsive efficiency is the amount of thrust developed by the _____ compared with the energy supplied to it in a usable form.

30. _____ efficiency is the amount of energy put into a usable form as compared to the total amount of energy available in the fuel.

31. _____ efficiency is the total heat released during the burning process, divided by the heat potential of the fuel burned.

32. _____ efficiency is defined as the heat value or heat energy output of the engine, divided by the heat energy input (fuel consumed).

33. The inlet area can be controlled by a set of vanes known as the _____ vanes.

34. There are two types of compressors with respect to airflow: the _____ type and the _____ type.

35. The compressor pressure ratio is the ratio of the air pressure at the compressor _____ to the air pressure at the compressor _____ .

36. The centrifugal compressor consists of three main parts: an _____ , a _____ , and a _____ .

37. In the term "centrifugal compressor," "centrifugal" means that the compressor is of the centrifugal type and that the air is compressed by _____ force.

38. The axial-flow compressor consists of two elements: a rotating member called the _____ ; and the _____ , which consists of rows of stationary blades.

39. A dual-compressor jet engine utilizes two separate compressors, each with its own driving _____ .

40. The forward compressor section is called the _____ -pressure compressor (N_1) and the rear section is called the _____ -pressure compressor (N_2).

41. The fan _____ is the amount of fan air (mass airflow) that flows through the fan duct compared with the airflow that flows through the core of the engine.

42. The failure of the compressor blades to move the air at the designed flow rate is called _____ .

43. The _____ of a typical gas-turbine engine is that portion of the air passage between the compressor and the combustion chamber or chambers.

44. The purpose of the diffuser is to reduce the _____ of the air and prepare it for entry into the combustion area.

45. Approximately 25% of the air that passes through the combustion section is actually used for combustion, the remaining air being used for _____ .

46. The cannular type of combustion chamber has characteristics of both the _____ and _____ types.

47. The turbine _____ is a series of airfoil-shaped vanes arranged in a ring at the rear of the combustion section of a gas-turbine engine.

48. The turbine vanes are exposed to the _____ temperatures in the engine.

49. Turbines come in three types: the _____ turbine, the _____ turbine, and a combination of the two called a _____ turbine.

50. A _____ turbine changes the speed and pressure of the gases.

51. The attachment of turbine blades to the turbine disk is usually accomplished by means of either _____ slots or _____ slots.

52. During most operating conditions, the nozzle exit velocity reaches the speed of sound, and the propelling nozzle is then said to be _____ —that is, no further increase in velocity can be obtained unless the _____ is increased.

53. The bypass engine has two gas streams to eject to the atmosphere: the _____ bypass airflow and the _____ turbine discharge gases.

54. The normal function of the exhaust nozzle, or cone, is to control the _____ and _____ of the exhaust gases.

55. Afterburners are used to greatly increase the thrust and therefore the speed of an aircraft for relatively short periods by increasing the _____ flow.

56. When combustion takes place in the afterburner, the gases are speeded up, increasing the _____ and _____ .

57. The two most commonly used types of thrust reversers are the _____ system and the _____ system.

58. The _____ section of a turbine engine is used to power engine and aircraft accessories such as fuel pumps.

59. The intensity of sound is measured in _____ .

60. The noise caused by the jet exhaust is termed "broadband noise" because it encompasses a wide range of _____ .

Chapter 11

Name _____

Date _____

APPLICATION QUESTIONS

1. Who was granted the first patent for a gas turbine engine? _____

2. What company made the first successful jet propelled flight? _____

3. What was the date of the flight referred to in the previous question? _____

4. List the types of jet propulsion engines.

    a. _____

    b. _____

    c. _____

    d. _____

5. List the types of gas-turbine engines.

    a. _____

    b. _____

    c. _____

    d. _____

    e. _____

6. State Newton's laws of motion.

    a. First law:

    _____

    _____

    _____

    b. Second law:

    _____

    _____

    _____

    c. Third law:

    _____

    _____

    _____

7. When airflow passes through a convergent duct,

    a. does its pressure increase or decrease? _____

    b. does its velocity increase or decrease? _____

8. When airflow passes through a divergent duct,

    a. does its pressure increase or decrease? _____

    b. does its velocity increase or decrease? _____

9. State the basic formula for calculating the approximate thrust of a gas-turbine engine. _____

10. What is the static thrust being developed by an engine operating with the following parameters?

_____

W_a = 15 lb/s

V_2 = 580 ft/s

V_1 = 0

W_f = 0.53 lb/s

V_j = 580 ft/s

11. An engine operating with the exhaust nozzle in a choked condition with the following parameters will develop how much net thrust? _____

W_a = 10 lb/s

V_2 = 485 ft/s

V_1 = 200 ft/s

W_f = 0.68 lb/s

V_j = 485 ft/s

A_j = 50 in^2

P_j = 17 lb/in^2

P_{amb} = 14 lb/in^2

12. What is the static thrust of an unchoked turbofan engine operating with the following parameters?

_____

Core engine:

W_a = 12 lb/s

V_2 = 312 ft/s

V_1 = 0

W_f = 0.75 lb/s

V_j = 312 lb/s

Fan:

W_a = 20 lb/s

V_2 = 160 ft/s

V_1 = 0

13. As an aircraft climbs, does thrust increase or decrease? _____

14. Define "propulsive efficiency."

_____

_____

15. List the two types of compressors used in gas-turbine engines.

    a. _____

    b. _____

16. Define "compressor stall."

_____

_____

_____

17. List the three types of combustion chambers used in gas-turbine engines.

    a. _____

    b. _____

    c. _____

18. List the three types of turbines.

    a. _____

    b. _____

    c. _____

19. Explain how a reaction-impulse turbine functions.

_____

_____

_____

20. List the two methods for attaching the turbine blades to the turbine disk.

    a. _____

    b. _____

21. What is the purpose of thrust reversers?

_____

_____

_____

22. List two advanced manufacturing processes used to produce gas-turbine engines.

    a. _____

    b. _____

Chapter 11

Name _____

Date _____

REVIEW EXAM

1. At what point in an axial-flow turbojet engine do the highest gas pressures occur?
   a. Immediately after the turbine section
   b. At the turbine entrance
   c. Within the burner section
   d. At the compressor outlet

2. Identify a function of the nozzle diaphragm in a turbojet engine.
   a. To decrease the velocity of exhaust gases
   b. To center the fuel spray in the combustion chamber
   c. To direct the flow of gases so as to strike the turbine buckets at a desired angle
   d. To direct the flow of gases into the combustion chamber

3. The fan rotational speed of a dual axial compressor forward fan engine is the same as that of the
   a. accessory drive shaft.
   b. low-pressure compressor.
   c. forward turbine wheel.
   d. high-pressure compressor.

4. What turbine-engine section provides for proper mixing of the fuel and air?
   a. Combustion section
   b. Compressor section
   c. Turbine section
   d. Accessory section

5. In a gas-turbine engine, combustion occurs at a constant
   a. volume.
   b. pressure.
   c. velocity.
   d. density.

6. Which of the following statements is true in regard to jet engines?
   a. At lower engine speeds, thrust increases rapidly with small increases in rpm.
   b. At higher engine speeds, thrust increases rapidly with small increases in rpm.
   c. Gas-turbine engines operate less efficiently at high altitudes because of the lower temperatures encountered.
   d. The thrust delivered per pound of air consumed is less at high altitude than at low altitude.

7. Where is the highest gas pressure in a turbojet engine?
   a. At the outlet of the tailpipe section
   b. At the entrance of the turbine section
   c. At the entrance of the burner section
   d. At the outlet of the burner section

8. An exhaust cone placed aft of the turbine in a gas-turbine engine will cause
   a. the pressure to increase and the velocity to decrease.
   b. the pressure to increase and the velocity to increase.
   c. the pressure to decrease and the velocity to increase.
   d. the pressure to decrease and the velocity to decrease.

9. What is the function of the stator vane assembly at the discharge end of a typical axial-flow compressor?
   a. To reduce drag on the first-stage turbine blades
   b. To straighten airflow to eliminate turbulence
   c. To direct the flow of gases into the combustion chambers
   d. To increase swirling of the air in the combustion chambers

10. The turbines near the rear of a jet engine
    a. compress air heated in the combustion section.
    b. increase air velocity for propulsion.
    c. circulate air to cool the engine.
    d. drive the compressor section.

11. In the dual axial-flow or twin-spool compressor system, the first-stage turbine drives the
    a. N_1 and N_2 compressors.
    b. N_3 compressor.
    c. N_2 compressor.
    d. N_1 compressor.

12. What are the two main sections of a turbine engine for inspection purposes?
    a. Combustion and exhaust
    b. Hot and cold
    c. Compressor and turbine
    d. Combustion and turbine

13. What are the two functional elements in a centrifugal compressor?
    a. Turbine and compressor
    b. Compressor and manifold
    c. Bucket and expander
    d. Impeller and diffuser

14. What is the most satisfactory method of attaching turbine blades to turbine wheels?
    a. The fir-tree design
    b. The tongue-and-groove design
    c. High-temperature, high-strength adhesive method
    d. Press fit method

15. A turbine-engine compressor which contains vanes on both sides of the impeller is a
    a. single-entry centrifugal compressor.
    b. double-entry centrifugal compressor.
    c. double-entry axial-flow compressor.
    d. single-entry axial-flow compressor.

16. How does a dual axial-flow compressor improve the efficiency of a turbojet engine?
    a. By allowing more turbine wheels to be used
    b. By reducing combustion chamber temperatures
    c. By allowing higher compression ratios to be obtained
    d. By increasing the velocity of the air entering the combustion chamber

17. Three types of turbine blades are
    a. reaction, converging, and diverging.
    b. impulse, reaction, and impulse-reaction.
    c. tangential, reaction, and reaction-tangential.
    d. impulse, vector, and impulse-vector.

18. An advantage of the axial-flow compressor is its
    a. low starting power requirements.
    b. low weight.
    c. high peak efficiency.
    d. high frontal area.

19. What is the purpose of the diffuser section in a turbine engine?
    a. To increase pressure and reduce velocity
    b. To speed up the airflow in the turbine section
    c. To convert pressure to velocity
    d. To reduce pressure and increase velocity

20. Which of the following are the most common types of thrust reversers used on turbine-engine-powered aircraft?
    a. Convergent and divergent
    b. Rotary air vane and stationary air vane
    c. Mechanical blockage and aerodynamic blockage
    d. Cascade vane and blocked door

21. Which of the following is the ultimate limiting factor of turbojet engine operation?
    a. Compressor inlet air temperature
    b. Compressor outlet air temperature
    c. Turbine inlet temperature
    d. Burner-can pressure

22. The highest heat-to-metal contact in a jet engine occurs in the
    a. burner cans.
    b. exhaust cone.
    c. turbine inlet guide vanes.
    d. turbine blades.

23. Which two elements make up the axial-flow compressor assembly?
    a. Rotor and stator
    b. Rotor and diffuser
    c. Compressor and manifold
    d. Stator and diffuser

24. As subsonic air flows through a convergent nozzle, its velocity
    a. increases.
    b. decreases.
    c. remains constant.
    d. is inversely proportional to the temperature.

25. As subsonic air flows through a convergent nozzle, its pressure
    a. increases.
    b. decreases.
    c. remains constant.
    d. is inversely proportional to the temperature.

26. The Brayton cycle is known as the constant
    a. pressure cycle.
    b. volume cycle.
    c. temperature cycle.
    d. mass cycle.

27. The exhaust section of a turbine engine is designed to
    a. impart a high exit velocity to the exhaust gases.
    b. swirl the exhaust gases.
    c. increase temperature, therefore increasing velocity.
    d. decrease temperature, therefore decreasing pressure.

28. Which of the following types of combustion sections are used in aircraft turbine engines?
    a. Variable, can-annular, and cascade vane
    b. Annular, variable, and cascade vane
    c. Can, multiple-can, and variable
    d. Multiple-can, annular, and can-annular

29. At what stage in a turbojet engine are pressures the greatest?
    a. Compressor inlet
    b. Turbine outlet
    c. Compressor outlet
    d. Tailpipe

30. In what section of a turbojet engine is the jet nozzle located?
    a. Combustion
    b. Turbine
    c. Compressor
    d. Exhaust

Chapter 12

STUDY QUESTIONS

1. Fuels generally available for use in turboprop and turbojet aircraft may be broadly categorized into two types:

   _____ and _____ gasolines.

2. Due to its greater density, kerosene has a _____ calorific or heating value per gallon than gasoline.

3. The vapor pressure of kerosene-type fuels is extremely _____ .

4. An advantage of wide-cut gasoline is its relatively _____ freezing point.

5. Turbine-engine fuels are _____ likely than gasoline to be contaminated with microorganisms.

6. The common turbine fuel system airframe components are:

   a. _____

   b. _____

   c. _____

   d. _____

7. The engine-mounted fuel system components in a typical system are:

   a. _____

   b. _____

   c. _____

   d. _____

   e. _____

   f. _____

8. The final components of the fuel system are the fuel _____ , which have as their essential function the task of atomizing or vaporizing the fuel to ensure its rapid burning.

9. The fuel filter has a _____ that will bypass fuel if the filter becomes clogged.

10. The _____ nozzle requires a primary and a main fuel manifold and has two independent orifices, one much smaller than the other.

11. The _____ nozzle carries a portion of the primary combustion air with the injected fuel.

12. A _____ blowout takes place when the mixture is too rich to burn.

13. If too little fuel enters the combustion chambers, a _____ die-out occurs.

14. The common parameters applied to the fuel control unit are:

   a. _____

   b. _____

   c. _____

   d. _____

   e. _____

15. Fuel control units which are hydraulic and mechanical in operation are called _____ .

Questions 16–20 apply to the FCU used on the Pratt & Whitney PT6A-60/65 series engines.

16. Control of N_g is accomplished by regulating the amount of fuel to the _____ section of the engine.

17. Compressor _____ pressure P_3 is sensed by the FCU and is used to establish acceleration fuel flow limits.

18. The fuel pressure immediately after the minimum flow orifice and the fuel valve is called _____ fuel pressure (P_2).

19. Engine speed is maintained by the _____ speed sensor (tachometer). Desired speed changes are set by the _____ , which determines the rotational position of the three-dimensional cam.

20. Engine speed N_g is directly proportional to _____ flow.

Questions 21–25 apply to the Hamilton Standard JFC68 fuel control unit.

21. The main units of the system are the:

   a. _____

   b. _____

   c. _____

22. The multiplying lever moves the throttle-valve pilot valve to direct _____ pressure, which moves the throttle valve.

23. Engine speed is controlled by the _____ . The governor continuously compares _____ engine speed N_2 with _____ speed, as selected by the pilot through the power lever.

24. The EVC3 engine vane control is designed to regulate the variable high-pressure compressor _____ of the engine by scheduling the position of the vanes in accordance with requirements dictated by the Mach number of compressor _____ airflow.

25. Varying the angle of the stator blades in accordance with the airflow velocity and temperature prevents _____ of the rotor blades and stator vanes.

Questions 26–29 apply to the Woodward fuel control unit.

26. The Woodward FCU is hydromechanical and is controlled by four parameters:

   a. _____

   b. _____

   c. _____

   d. _____

27. Fuel metering in the Woodward FCU is accomplished by means of a _____ fuel metering port across which is maintained a constant pressure differential.

28. When the flyweight centrifugal force and the speeder spring force are balanced, the engine is in an _____ condition.

29. If the engine is not on speed, the governor will direct pressure to or from the governor _____ to change the opening of the fuel metering port.

30. An electronic engine fuel control that receives information regarding various engine operating parameters and adjusts a standard hydromechanical FCU to obtain the most effective engine operation is called a _____ EEC.

31. The _____ EEC is a system that receives all the necessary data for engine operation and develops the commands to various actuators to control the engine parameters within the limits required for the most efficient and safe engine operation.

Chapter 12

Name _____

Date _____

APPLICATION QUESTIONS

1. List the qualities that a gas-turbine fuel should have.

   a. _____

   b. _____

   c. _____

   d. _____

   e. _____

   f. _____

   g. _____

   h. _____

2. List two different types of jet fuel.

   a. _____

   b. _____

3. List two problems associated with the presence of water in the fuel.

   a. _____

   b. _____

4. Define a "duplex nozzle."

   _____

   _____

5. Some of the engine conditions or parameters that are sensed by gas-turbine engine fuel system controllers are:

   a. _____

   b. _____

   c. _____

   d. _____

   e. _____

6. Describe the full authority EEC system or controller.

   _____

   _____

   _____

Chapter 12

REVIEW EXAM

1. In-flight turbine-engine flameouts are usually caused by
   a. high exhaust-gas temperature.
   b. interruption of the inlet airflow.
   c. fouling of the primary igniter plugs.
   d. fuel-nozzle clogging.

2. Which of the following influences the operation of an automatic fuel control unit on a turbojet engine?
   a. Fuel temperature
   b. Burner pressure
   c. Mixture control position
   d. Exhaust-gas temperature

3. Which of the following is a function of the fuel-oil heat exchanger on a turbojet engine?
   a. To remove oil vapors
   b. To aerate the fuel
   c. To emulsify the oil
   d. To increase fuel temperature

4. Which type of fuel control is used on most of today's turbine engines?
   a. Electromechanical
   b. Mechanical
   c. Hydromechanical or electronic
   d. Hydraulic

5. What are the positions of the pressurization valve and the dump valve in a jet engine fuel system when the engine is shut down?
   a. Pressurization valve open, dump valve closed
   b. Pressurization valve closed, dump valve open
   c. Pressurization valve open, dump valve open
   d. Pressurization valve closed, dump valve closed

6. Which of the following is *not* an input parameter for a turbine-engine fuel control unit?
   a. Engine or high-pressure compressor rotor speed.
   b. Compressor inlet pressure.
   c. Compressor inlet temperature.
   d. Ambient humidity.

7. Consider the following statements.
   (1) A supervisory electronic engine control (EEC) is a system that receives information regarding various engine operating parameters and adjusts a standard hydromechanical fuel control unit to obtain the most effective engine operation.
   (2) A full-authority EEC is a system that receives all the necessary data for engine operations and develops the commands to various actuators to control engine parameters.
   Of these two statements,

   a. both No. 1 and No. 2 are true.
   b. neither No. 1 nor No. 2 is true.
   c. only No. 1 is true.
   d. only No. 2 is true.

8. The primary condition that allows microorganisms to grow in fuel is
   a. warm temperatures.
   b. the absence of light.
   c. the presence of water.
   d. the presence of dirt or other particulate contaminants.

9. What is the purpose of the flow divider in a turbine-engine duplex fuel nozzle?
   a. To allow an alternate flow of fuel if the primary flow clogs or is restricted
   b. To direct excessive fuel back to the fuel manifold
   c. To create the primary and secondary fuel supplies
   d. To provide a flow path for bleed air which aids in the atomization of fuel

10. What causes the fuel divider valve to open in a turbine-engine duplex fuel nozzle?
    a. Fuel pressure
    b. Thermostatically controlled heat from the combustion section
    c. Bleed air after the engine reaches idle rpm
    d. An electrically operated solenoid

Chapter 13

STUDY QUESTIONS

1. Lubricating oils for gas-turbine engines are usually of the _____ type.

2. Synthetic lubricants have a high _____ characteristic which allows them to penetrate and dissolve paints, enamels, and other materials.

3. When changing or adding oil to a gas-turbine engine system, the technician must be certain that a lubricant of the correct _____ and _____ is used.

4. The pressure oil pump is generally a _____ -type pump.

5. Gas-turbine lubrication systems are usually of the _____ type, in that the oil is scavenged from the engine and stored in an oil tank.

6. A _____ oil pump returns oil from the engine's bearing cavities to a sump in an accessory drive gearbox or directly to the oil tank.

7. A scavenge oil pump is normally of a _____ capacity than the engine-driven pump because of the air that mixes with the oil (foaming) in the bearing cavities.

8. The size of the filter mesh is measured in _____ .

9. A _____ detector indicates the presence of metal contamination without the need for the filter to be opened.

10. In turbine-engine oil systems, the two types of oil coolers employed are _____ -cooled oil coolers and ram _____ oil coolers.

11. An oil _____ system removes oil droplets and vapor by a centrifugal separator located in the accessory drive gearbox.

12. There are three basic oil circulating systems, known as a _____ system, a _____ system, and a _____ system.

13. In the _____ system, the oil flow to the bearing chambers is controlled by limiting the pressure in the feed line to a given value.

14. The _____ system does not utilize a relief valve and achieves the desired oil flow rates throughout the complete engine speed range by allowing the pressure-pump delivery pressure to go directly to the oil feed jets.

15. A _____ oil system works on the principle that once the oil has been used for bearing lubrication it is disposed of; there is no recirculation.

16. Oil _____ is an analytical process which, when used within certain limits, can identify some engine problems before major engine damage or failure occurs.

17. The two most common methods for analyzing wear metals are _____ and _____ .

Chapter 13

Name _____

Date _____

APPLICATION QUESTIONS

1. What type of oil is used in a gas-turbine engine? _____

2. List three different types of lubricating systems used on gas-turbine engines.

   a. _____

   b. _____

   c. _____

3. Describe a magnetic chip detector.

   _____

   _____

4. Describe a labyrinth seal and explain its operation.

   _____

   _____

   _____

   _____

5. During an oil analysis program, what is indicated by a sudden increase in wear metals of a particular type?

   _____

Chapter 13

Name _____

Date _____

REVIEW EXAM

1. In regard to using a turbine-engine oil analysis program, which of the following is false?
   a. Generally, an accurate trend forecast may be made after an engine's first oil sample analysis.
   b. It is best to start an oil analysis program on an engine when it is new.
   c. A successful oil analysis program should be run over an engine's total operating life so that normal trends can be established.
   d. Engines that are not new may be started on an oil analysis program with at least a moderate degree of success.

2. Oil picks up the most heat from which of the following turbojet engine components?
   a. Rotor coupling
   b. Compressor bearing
   c. Accessory drive bearing
   d. Turbine bearing

3. Main-bearing oil seals used with turbine engines are usually of what type(s)?
   a. Labryinth and/or carbon rubbing
   b. Silicone rubber and nylon
   c. Teflon and synthetic rubber
   d. Labryinth and/or silicone rubber

4. What type of oil system is usually found on a turbojet engine?
   a. Dry sump, pressure, and spray
   b. Wet sump, dip, and pressure
   c. Dry sump, dip, and splash
   d. Wet sump, spray, and splash

5. Why are synthetic lubricants used in high-performance turbine engines?
   a. Synthetic oils do not require filtering and are less expensive.
   b. The load-carrying characteristics of petroleum-base oils have a low degree of chemical stability.
   c. Additives required in turbine engines cannot be mixed with petroleum oils.
   d. Synthetic oils have less tendency to produce lacquer or coke and less tendency to evaporate at high temperatures.

6. The oil pumps of the type most commonly used on turbine engines are classified as
   a. positive-displacement pumps.
   b. variable-displacement pumps.
   c. constant-speed pumps.
   d. fixed-pressure pumps.

7. Consider the following statements.
   (1) Fuel may be used to cool oil in gas-turbine engines.
   (2) Ram air may be used to cool oil in gas-turbine engines.
   Of these two statements,
   a. only No. 1 is true.
   b. only No. 2 is true.
   c. neither No. 1 nor No. 2 is true.
   d. both No. 1 and No. 2 are true.

8. The main-bearing oil-damper compartments found in some turbine engines are used primarily to
   a. provide lubrication of bearings from the beginning of starting rotation until normal oil pressure is established.
   b. keep carbon seals lubricated with engine oil in order to prevent a "dry" rubbing condition and leakage during an engine start.
   c. provide an oil film between the outer race and the bearing housing in order to reduce vibration tendencies in the rotor system.
   d. prevent surges in oil pressure to the bearings.

9. In a jet engine which uses a fuel-oil heat exchanger, the oil temperature is controlled by a thermostatic valve that regulates the flow of
   a. air past the heat exchanger.
   b. fuel through the heat exchanger.
   c. both fuel and oil through the heat exchanger.
   d. oil through the heat exchanger.

10. Possible failure-related ferrous-metal particles in turbine-engine oil cause an (electrical) indicating-type magnetic chip detector to indicate their presence by
   a. disturbing the eddy currents around the detector tip.
   b. disturbing the magnetic lines of flux about the detector tip.
   c. bridging the gap between the detector center (positive) electrode and the ground electrode.
   d. generating a small electric current that is caused by contact between the particles and the dissimilar metal of the detector tip.

11. What would be the probable result if the pressure relief valve in the oil system of a turbine engine should stick in the open position?
   a. Increased oil pressure
   b. Decreased oil temperature
   c. Insufficient lubrication
   d. Pressurization of the case and increased oil leakage

12. What is the primary purpose of the oil-to-fuel heat exchanger?
   a. To cool the fuel
   b. To cool the oil
   c. To deaerate the oil
   d. To decrease the viscosity of the oil

13. The purpose of directing bleed air to the bearings in a turbine engine is to
   a. increase oil pressure at the bearings.
   b. provide a high volume of oil flow across the bearings.
   c. warm cold engine oil quickly.
   d. aid in removing heat from the bearings.

14. Consider the following statements.
   (1) Wet-sump oil systems are most commonly used in gas-turbine engines.
   (2) Oil in gas-turbine engines is not diluted during cold weather.
   Of these two statements,
   a. only No. 1 is true.
   b. both No. 1 and No. 2 are true.
   c. only No. 2 is true.
   d. neither No. 1 nor No. 2 is true.

15. A turbine-engine dry-sump lubrication system of the self-contained, high-pressure design
   a. uses the same storage area as a wet-sump engine.
   b. has no heat exchanger.
   c. consists of pressure, breather, and scavenge subsystems.
   d. stores oil in the engine crankcase.

Chapter 14

STUDY QUESTIONS

1. Ignition systems for gas-turbine engines consist of three main components, the _____ , the _____ , and the _____ .

2. The exciter box provides a high voltage to the _____ , which transfers the high voltage to the igniter.

3. The igniter is mounted in the engine in such a way as to allow it to protrude into the _____ section of the engine.

4. When the system is activated, the exciter creates a high voltage which is discharged across the igniter _____ and ignites the _____ inside the engine's combustion section during starting.

5. Ignition systems for gas-turbine engines are required to operate for _____ only.

6. An important characteristic of a gas-turbine ignition system is the _____ discharge at the igniter plug.

7. The high-energy discharge is accomplished by means of a storage capacitor in what is termed a high-energy _____ system.

8. Under certain flight conditions, it may be necessary for the ignition system to operate continuously so that it can provide an automatic relight should a _____ occur.

9. A _____ system, used on some models of gas-turbine engines, provides current to a hot coil element in each plug which makes the plug glow red hot.

10. The igniter is made up of four basic parts: _____ , _____ , _____ , and _____ .

11. In some cases the igniter must also operate during aircraft operational modes in order to ensure a restart if the engine should flame out. This ignition state, generally called _____ ignition, provides a _____ spark to one igniter plug.

12. All igniters, except the glow-plug variety, emit a sharp _____ noise when firing.

13. When servicing ignitors do not, under any circumstances, remove any deposits or residue from the firing end of _____ -voltage igniters.

14. The most commonly used type of starter is the _____ starter.

15. The two types of air-turbine starters are the _____ starter and the _____ starter.

16. The low-pressure air-turbine starter is designed to operate with a _____ -volume, _____ -pressure air supply.

17. The two principal types of combustion starters are the _____ starter and the _____ starter.

18. A _____ starter is used for some jet engines and is completely self-contained. It has its own fuel and ignition system, its own starting system, and a self-contained oil system.

Chapter 14

APPLICATION QUESTIONS

1. When is a gas-turbine engine ignition system normally used?

   _____

2. List the three major components of a turbine-engine ignition system.

   a. _____

   b. _____

   c. _____

3. Define the term "igniter."

   _____

   _____

4. How long should it normally take for a glow plug to heat up to a bright yellow color? _____

5. Starting systems for gas-turbine engines fall into two major categories. List them.

   a. _____

   b. _____

6. What energy source is normally used to start large turbofan engines on airliners? _____

7. List the three sources of the compressed air that is normally used to start large turbofan engines.

   a. _____

   b. _____

   c. _____

8. Define the term "auxiliary power unit."

   _____

   _____

9. What two things does the APU normally supply for the aircraft while on the ground?

   a. _____

   b. _____

Chapter 14

Name _____

Date _____

REVIEW EXAM

1. The capacitor-type ignition system is used almost universally on turbine engines because of its high voltage and
   a. low amperage.
   b. long life.
   c. low temperature range.
   d. high heat intensity.

2. How does the ignition system of a gas-turbine engine differ from that of a reciprocating engine?
   a. One igniter plug is used in each combustion chamber.
   b. Low-energy igniter plugs are used in place of spark plugs.
   c. Magneto-to-engine timing is not critical.
   d. A high-energy spark is required for ignition.

3. In a turbine-engine dc capacitor discharge ignition system, where are the high-voltage pulses formed?
   a. At the breaker
   b. At the triggering transformer
   c. At the rectifier
   d. At the multilobe cam

4. Why are turbine-engine igniters less susceptible to fouling than reciprocating-engine spark plugs?
   a. The high-intensity spark cleans the igniter with heat.
   b. The frequency of the spark is lower for igniters.
   c. Turbine igniters operate at lower temperatures.
   d. Turbine fuel does not contain igniter contaminants.

5. The constrained-gap igniter plug used in some gas-turbine engines operates at a lower temperature because
   a. it projects into the combustion chamber.
   b. the applied voltage is less.
   c. the construction is such that the spark occurs beyond the face of the combustion chamber liner.
   d. it has multiple electrodes to share the voltage arcing.

6. When a turbine-engine igniter plug is removed, in order to eliminate the possibility of the technician receiving a lethal shock, the ignition switch is turned off. In addition to this precaution,
   a. the ignition switch should be disconnected from the power-supply circuit.
   b. insulating rubber gloves should be worn.
   c. the igniter lead should be disconnected from the plug and the center electrode grounded to the engine after the transformer-exciter input lead has been disconnected from the plug and the prescribed waiting period observed.
   d. the transformer-exciter input lead should be disconnected from the plug and the center electrode grounded to the engine after the igniter lead has been disconnected from the plug and the prescribed waiting period observed.

7. Igniter plugs used in turbine engines are subjected to much higher voltage than reciprocating-engine spark plugs, and yet their service life is longer. This is because
   a. they operate at much lower temperatures.
   b. their electrode gap is much smaller.
   c. they are not placed directly in the combustion area.
   d. they are not required to operate continuously.

8. Which statement is correct in regard to the ignition system of a turbojet engine?
   a. The system is normally deenergized as soon as the engine starts.
   b. It is a low-voltage, high-amperage system.
   c. It is energized during the starting and warm-up periods only.
   d. The system generally includes a polar inductor-type magneto.

9. The type of ignition system used on most turbine aircraft engines is a
   a. high-resistance system.
   b. magneto system.
   c. low-tension system.
   d. capacitor-discharge system.

10. Why do turbine-engine ignition systems require high
energy?
   a. For ignition of the fuel under conditions of high
      altitude and high temperatures.
   b. Because the applied voltage is very high.
   c. For ignition of the fuel under conditions of high
      altitude and low temperatures.
   d. Because the applied voltage is very low.

Chapter 15

STUDY QUESTIONS

1. The Pratt & Whitney JT8D is a _____ -spool _____ -flow gas-turbine engine.

2. The JT8D engine has six general sections. These are the _____ section, the _____ section, the _____ section, the _____ and _____ section, the _____ drives, and the _____ section.

3. The JT8D _____ section is the most forward section of the engine.

4. The purpose of the _____ vanes is to direct the incoming air at the proper angle to the first fan stage.

5. The front-compressor section and the fan section of the JT8D engine are both part of the same rotating assembly. The fan is actually the outer ends of the first _____ compressor blades.

6. In the JT8D engine, the primary air and secondary air are almost equally divided by _____ .

7. The JT8D front compressor is driven by the second, third, and fourth turbine stages through the _____ drive shaft.

8. The JT8D rear (N_2) compressor is driven by the _____ -stage turbine.

9. Each of the JT8D rotor-disk spacers has two knife-edge air seals on its outer diameter. The purpose of the knife-edge seals is to prevent _____ between stages.

10. In the JT8D, two rows of radial, straightening exit-guide vanes at the entrance to the diffuser case slow the circular whirl pattern and convert the whirl-velocity energy to _____ energy.

11. A gradually increasing cross section of the JT8D difusser air passage _____ the velocity of the airflow and at the same time converts the _____ energy to pressure energy.

12. In the JT8D, combustion chambers _____ and _____ each have a spark-igniter opening.

13. In the JT8D, the turbine blade tips form a complete ring or shroud to reduce gas _____ .

14. In the JT8D, the blades for the second, third, and fourth turbines are secured in the disks by _____ slots and rivets.

15. The JT9D fan section bypasses more than _____ times as much air as passes through the core of the cngine.

16. The JT9D is a _____ -spool engine, driving the fan and low-pressure compressor by means of the _____ most rearward turbine stages through the center coaxial shaft.

17. The JT9D high-pressure compressor is driven by the _____ most forward turbine stages.

18. The five rotating modules of the JT9D are the _____ assembly, the _____ assembly, the _____ assembly, the _____ assembly, and the _____ assembly.

19. When the JT9D engine is assembled, there are only two principal rotating assemblies. These may be termed the fan and _____ -pressure compressor and the drive turbine and _____ -pressure compressor.

20. In the JT9D engine, each stage of vanes in the high-pressure compressor is operated through a

_____ ring, which makes all vanes in the stage rotate the same amount.

21. The combustion chamber of the JT9D engine is a two-piece _____ chamber with both inner and outer liners.

22. The Pratt & Whitney 2037 is a _____ -rotor, high-bypass-ratio, _____ -flow turbofan engine.

23. In the PW2037 engine, the single-stage fan and four-stage low-pressure compressor are driven by a

_____ -stage turbine at the rear of the engine. The twelve-stage high-pressure compressor is driven by a _____ -stage turbine.

24. The PW4000 incorporates an active clearance control (ACC) which controls the clearances between the

_____ blade tips and the _____ case.

25. The General Electric CF6-50 engine fan section includes the _____ compressor stages which may be defined as the low-pressure compressor.

26. The annular combustor for the CF6 engine consists of four sections: the _____ assembly, which serves as a diffuser; the _____ ; the _____ skirt; and the

_____ skirt.

27. The high-pressure turbine (HPT) of the CF6 engine consists of _____ stages.

28. The General Electric CFM56-3 engine has _____ major modules that can be separated from the assembly to perform specific maintenance operations. The three major modules are the _____ major module, the _____ engine major module, and the _____ major module.

29. The Rolls-Royce RB 211 engine is a _____ -shaft engine.

30. The RB 211 three-shaft configuration is employed to permit the _____ to rotate independently so that it will not limit the optimum rotational speed of the _____ compressor.

31. The RB 211 fan is driven by the rearmost three stages of the turbine through the _____ coaxial shaft.

32. The RB 211 high-pressure compressor is driven by the _____ stage of the turbine through the

_____ of the three coaxial shafts.

33. The RB 211 combustion chamber is a short, annular chamber fitted with _____ fuel nozzles.

34. The HPT blades of the RB 211 engine are _____ -cooled by air bled from the high-pressure compressor.

35. The Garrett TFE731 fan is driven through a _____ to avoid overspeeding and yet allow the low-pressure compressor to operate at the most efficient speed.

36. On the TFE731 engine, a part of the fan output is directed inward to the _____ -pressure compressor; therefore, the fan provides a first stage of compression.

37. The TFE731 low-pressure compressor assembly has _____ axial-flow compressor rotors shafted to, and driven by, a _____ -stage axial-flow LPT assembly.

38. On the TFE731 engine, a single-stage _____ compressor impeller shafted to, and driven by, a single-stage _____ -flow turbine wheel comprises the high-pressure compressor assembly.

39. The Garrett ATF3-6 is a _____ -spool engine with separate turbines to drive the fan, low-pressure compressor, and high-pressure compressor.

40. On the ATF3-6 engine, air leaving the low-pressure compressor is split into eight ducts and is carried to the rear of the engine where it is turned _____ ° and directed to the inlet of the _____ -pressure compressor.

41. The ATF3-6 burner is a _____ -flow type in which the gas-flow changes direction approximately 180°.

42. The type of engine design which simplifies maintenance by making it possible to remove sections for repair or overhaul without having to disassemble the complete engine is called _____ construction.

Chapter 15

Name _____

Date _____

APPLICATION QUESTIONS

1. List three aircraft that use the JT8D engine.

    a. _____

    b. _____

    c. _____

2. What is the latest series of the Pratt & Whitney JT8D engine? _____

3. How many compressors does the Pratt & Whitney JT9D engine have? _____

4. List three aircraft that are powered by the Pratt & Whitney JT9D-7R4 engine?

    a. _____

    b. _____

    c. _____

5. With regard to the Pratt & Whitney 2037 turbofan engine, what is the normal takeoff thrust sea level static?

    _____

6. What is the thrust range of the Pratt & Whitney PW4000 engine? _____

7. List the three basic dash numbers of the General Electric CF6 series of engines.

    a. _____

    b. _____

    c. _____

8. What two aircraft can be powered by the General Electric CF6-80 engine?

    a. _____

    b. _____

9. How many compressors are there in the Rolls-Royce RB 211? _____

10. In the Garrett TFE731 engine, what unit directly drives the fan and reduces the rpm? _____

11. What type of combustion chamber does the Pratt & Whitney JT15D engine incorporate? _____

Chapter 15

Name _____

Date _____

REVIEW EXAM

1. What is the purpose of the stator blades in the compressor section of a turbine engine?
   a. To stabilize pressure
   b. To prevent compressor surge
   c. To control direction of the airflow
   d. To increase velocity of the airflow

2. In which type of turbine-engine combustion chamber are the case and liner removed and installed as one unit during routine maintenance?
   a. Can
   b. Can-annular
   c. Variable
   d. Annular

3. The diffuser section of a jet aircraft engine is located between
   a. the burner section and the turbine section.
   b. the N_1 section and the N_2 section.
   c. station No. 7 and station No. 8.
   d. the compressor section and the burner section.

4. Reduced blade vibration and improved airflow characteristics in gas turbines are brought about by
   a. fir-tree blade attachment.
   b. impulse-type blades.
   c. shrouded turbine rotor blades.
   d. bulb root attachment.

5. Which turbine-engine compressor offers the greatest advantages for both starting flexibility and improved high-altitude performance?
   a. Single-stage, centrifugal-flow
   b. Dual-stage, centrifugal-flow
   c. Split-spool, axial-flow
   d. Single-spool, axial-flow

6. The two types of compressors most commonly used in jet engines are
   a. axial and root.
   b. centrifugal and reciprocating.
   c. root and centrifugal.
   d. centrifugal and axial.

7. In a dual axial-flow compressor, the first-stage turbine drives
   a. the N_2 compressor.
   b. the N_1 compressor.
   c. the low-pressure compressor.
   d. both low- and high-pressure compressors.

8. What is used in turbine engines to aid in stabilization of compressor airflow during low-thrust engine operation?
   a. Stator vanes and rotor vanes
   b. Variable guide vanes and/or compressor bleed valves
   c. Pressurization and dump valves
   d. Variable geometry inlet ducts

9. In a turbine engine with a dual-spool compressor, the low-speed compressor
   a. always turns at the same speed as the high-speed compressor.
   b. is connected directly to the high-speed compressor.
   c. seeks its own best operating speed.
   d. has a higher compressor shaft speed than the high-speed compressor.

10. What is the function of the inlet guide vane assembly on an axial-flow compressor?
    a. To direct the air into the first-stage rotor blades at the proper angle
    b. To convert velocity energy into pressure energy
    c. To convert pressure energy into velocity energy
    d. To pick up air and increase its energy by accelerating it outward by centrifugal force

11. A gas-turbine engine comprises which three main sections?
    a. Compressor, diffuser, and scavenge
    b. Turbine, combustion, and scavenge
    c. Combustion, compressor, and inlet guide vane
    d. Compressor, combustion, and turbine

12. What type of turbine blade is most commonly used in aircraft jet engines?
    a. Reaction
    b. Divergent
    c. Impulse
    d. Reaction-impulse

13. What is the primary factor which controls the pressure ratio of an axial-flow compressor?
    a. Number of stages in compressor
    b. Rotor diameter
    c. Compressor inlet pressure
    d. Compressor inlet temperature

14. Consider the following statements.
    (1) A turbine-engine axial-flow compressor is made up of a series of rotating airfoils called rotor blades and a stationary set of airfoils called stator vanes.
    (2) In a turbine engine, a row of rotating and stationary blades is called a stage.
    Of these two statements,

    a. only No. 1 is true.
    b. only No. 2 is true.
    c. both No. 1 and No. 2 are true.
    d. neither No. 1 nor No. 2 is true.

15. Consider the following statements.
    (1) In a turbine-engine axial-flow compressor, each consecutive pair of rotor and stator blades constitutes a pressure stage.
    (2) In a turbine-engine axial-flow compressor, the number of rows of stages is determined by the amount of air and total pressure rise required.
    Of these two statements,

    a. only No. 1 is true.
    b. only No. 2 is true.
    c. both No. 1 and No. 2 are true.
    d. neither No. 1 nor No. 2 is true.

Chapter 16

STUDY QUESTIONS

1. Although various names have been applied to gas-turbine and propeller combinations, the most widely used name is _____ .

2. In a turboprop engine, the compressor, the combustion section, and the compressor turbine comprise what is often called the gas _____ or gas _____ .

3. The gas generator produces the high-velocity gases which drive the _____ .

4. A _____ turbine is not mechanically connected to the gas generator.

5. In a _____ shaft turbine engine, the shaft is mechanically connected to the gearbox.

6. The gear reduction from the engine to the propeller is of a much _____ ratio than that used in a reciprocating engine because of the high rpm of the gas-turbine engine.

7. The propeller pitch and the fuel flow must be coordinated in order to maintain the constant-speed condition. When fuel flow is decreased, _____ pitch must also be decreased.

8. The Rolls-Royce Dart turboprop engine utilizes a _____ -entry _____ -stage centrifugal compressor, a _____ -type through-flow combustion section, and a _____ -stage turbine.

9. On the Dart engine, the interconnectors are necessary to equalize the gas _____ and provide a means of passing the _____ during light-up.

10. On the Dart engine, the oil cooler discharges into the oil tank, where the oil is directed over a deaerator tray which spreads it out thinly to permit the release of included _____ .

11. The Dart engine has a system in which water and methanol from the aircraft tank are injected into the first-stage _____ through drilled passages in the rotating guide vanes and impeller.

12. The Pratt & Whitney 100 series turboprop engine has an annular _____ -flow combustion chamber.

13. On the P&W 100, the engine fuel flow is controlled by the _____ lever and the _____ lever through two integrated systems: the _____ control system and the _____ control system.

14. On the P&W 100, the electronic components of the fuel control system are the _____ signal conditioner and the engine _____ control.

15. The P&W 100 has a transfer tube located in the propeller shaft which conveys the oil from the PCU to the propeller _____ mechanism.

16. The General Electric CT7 turboprop engine features modular construction with a _____ -spool gas generator section consisting of a _____ -stage axial compressor and a single-stage _____ -flow compressor; a low-fuel-pressure through-flow _____ combustion chamber; an air-cooled, _____ -stage, axial-flow high-pressure turbine; and a _____ two-stage, uncooled, axial-flow power turbine.

17. The CT7 turboprop engine power unit consists of four modules: the _____ module, the _____ section module, the _____ section module, and the _____ module.

18. The CT7 electrical control unit has four basic functions: power-turbine _____ protection, control of minimum power-turbine speed during _____ operation, control of constant torque on _____ , and cockpit indication of _____ , _____ , and _____ .

19. The CT7 propeller system operates in two modes: the _____ mode, for normal flight conditions, and the _____ control mode, for taxiing and reverse thrust.

20. The beta range is from the _____ position to the _____ position.

Questions 21–39 refer to the PT6A turboprop engine.

21. The PT6A engine is described as a lightweight, _____ -turbine engine.

22. The inlet air intake is screened to preclude the ingestion of _____ .

23. The compressor rotor and stator assembly consists of a three-stage _____ rotor, three interstage spacers, _____ stators, and a single-stage _____ impeller and housing.

24. The gas generator case is attached to the front flange of the compressor inlet case and encloses both the _____ and the _____ section.

25. The combustion-chamber liner is a _____ -flow liner and consists primarily of an _____ , heat-resistant steel liner.

26. The direction of airflow in the combustion chamber is controlled by _____ rings, especially those located opposite the perforations.

27. The turbine rotor section consists of two separate _____ -stage turbines located in the center of the gas generator case.

28. The two turbines are mounted on shafts which extend in _____ directions. The rear shaft drives the _____ , and the forward shaft drives the _____ through the reduction-gear assembly.

29. This turbine drives the compressor in a _____ direction.

30. A squealer tip is designed to cause a minimum amount of pickup if the blade should come into contact with the _____ segments during operation.

31. The compressor turbine is separated from the power turbine by an _____ which prevents dissipation of turbine gases.

32. The power-turbine disk assembly drives the reduction gearing through the power-turbine shaft in a _____ direction.

33. The PT6A engine is equipped with a gearbox at the front for the reduction of engine speed to a level suitable for driving a _____ . The reduction gear ratio is _____ .

34. A _____ is used to determine the torque force being exerted by the engine.

35. The value indicated by the torquemeter is used to determine _____ output.

36. The PT6A engine has three separate air-bleed systems: a _____ bleed control, a _____ air seal and bleed system, and a _____ cooling system.

37. The compressor- and power-turbine disks are both cooled by _____ discharge air.

38. Some PT6A engines include a fuel heater through which the fuel is heated by engine _____ .

39. The PT6A engine employs _____ plugs for ignition rather than the high-energy spark ignitors.

40. The Garrett TPE331 engine is a single-spool engine; that is, it has one main rotating assembly that includes both the _____ and the _____ .

41. The TPE331 engine has a two-stage _____ compressor located on the main shaft in the forward section of the engine.

42. To the rear of the compressor section in the TPE331 engine is the _____ -stage turbine that extracts power from the hot, high-velocity gases and delivers the power through the main shaft to both the _____ and the _____ reduction gears.

43. On the TPE331, when a negative torque signal (NTS) is produced, the system automatically _____ the propeller to stop engine rotation and reduce drag.

Chapter 16

Name _____

Date _____

APPLICATION QUESTIONS

1. Describe the free-turbine turboprop engine.

   _____

   _____

2. Describe the fixed shaft turboprop engine.

   _____

   _____

   _____

3. The gas generator or gas producer of a turboprop engine consists of what three components?

   a. _____

   b. _____

   c. _____

4. In the Pratt & Whitney 100 series turboprop engine, what is another name for the turbo machine?

   _____

5. Describe the modular construction features of the General Electric CT7 turboprop engine.

   _____

   _____

   _____

   _____

6. List the levers that are normally used with the CT7 engine.

   a. _____

   b. _____

7. Is the Pratt & Whitney PT6A turboprop engine a free-turbine engine or a fixed-turbine engine?

   _____

8. List two of the aircraft that use the PT6A turboprop engine.

   a. _____

   b. _____

9. Identify the components indicated in the diagram below.

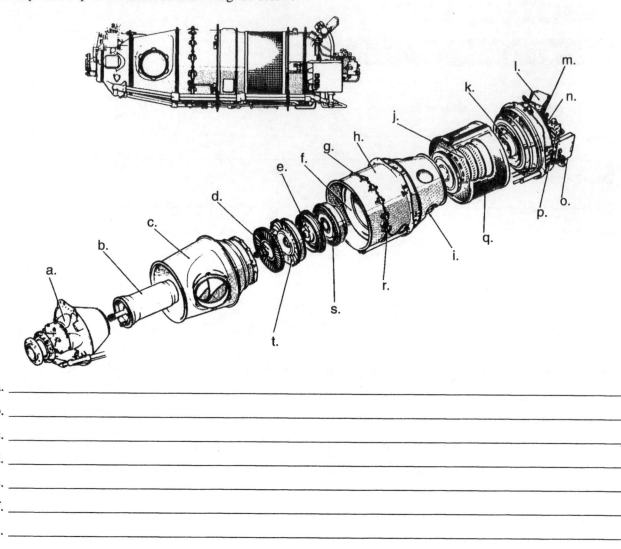

a. _____

b. _____

c. _____

d. _____

e. _____

f. _____

g. _____

h. _____

i. _____

j. _____

k. _____

l. _____

m. _____

n. _____

o. _____

p. _____

q. _____

r. _____

s. _____

t. _____

10. How many compressor stages are used in the Garrett TPE331 turboprop engine? _____

11. What type of compressors are used in the TPE331 engine? _____

12. How many turbine stages are used in the TPE331 engine? _____

Chapter 16

Name _____

Date _____

REVIEW EXAM

1. A turboprop powerplant propeller
   a. is governed at the same speed as that of the turbine.
   b. controls the speed of the engine in the beta range.
   c. accounts for 75 to 85% of the total thrust output.
   d. accounts for 15 to 25% of the total thrust output.

2. The gas generator or gas producer of a free-turbine turboprop engine produces
   a. electricity.
   b. thrust.
   c. high-velocity gases which drive the power turbine.
   d. high-velocity gases which drive a fixed-shaft turbine.

3. The PW100 series engine is used on which of the following commuter aircraft?
   a. Aerospatiale ATR
   b. British Aerospace ATP
   c. DeHavilland Dash 8
   d. All of these

4. In the Pratt & Whitney PT6A engine, what is the total number of degrees of bend (turns) that the airflow undergoes from the time the air enters the engine until it exits the exhaust?
   a. 900°
   b. 720°
   c. 360°
   d. 440°

5. The combustion-chamber liner in the Pratt & Whitney PT6A engine is a
   a. can type.
   b. can-annular type.
   c. annular reverse-flow type.
   d. axial straight-flow type.

6. What type of compressor assembly does the PT6A employ?
   a. Three-stage axial
   b. Two-stage centrifugal
   c. Three-stage axial, one-stage centrifugal
   d. Five-stage axial

7. How many compressor-turbine stages are there in the PT6A?
   a. 2
   b. 3
   c. 4
   d. 1

8. What kind of starter is used on the PT6A?
   a. Air turbine
   b. Combustion
   c. Electric starter-generator
   d. Hand starter

9. What does the PT6A engine use to ignite the fuel for starting?
   a. Spark plugs
   b. High-tension ignition system
   c. Magnetos
   d. Two glow plugs

10. What is the purpose of the free-power turbine in the PT6A?
    a. To turn the compressor
    b. To pump fuel
    c. To drive the gearbox and propeller
    d. To provide cabin air pressure

Chapter 17

1. A gas-turbine engine that delivers power through a shaft to operate something other than a propeller is referred to as a _____ engine.

2. The shaft turbine may produce some thrust, but it is primarily designed to produce _____ .

3. Small gas-turbine engines used mostly on large transport aircraft for providing auxiliary power either on the ground or in flight if needed are called _____ .

4. APUs normally operate at about _____ % rpm.

5. The Garrett GTCP APU is composed of three distinct modules: the _____ , the _____ , and the _____ .

6. The power section of the GTCP APU is a single-shaft gas-turbine engine which converts air and fuel into _____ horsepower.

7. The GTCP APU load compressor, which is driven by the power section, supplies _____ for the airplane's pneumatic system.

8. On the GTCP APU, the gearbox, which is also driven by the _____ section, contains gears and drive pads for the various APU accessories, including the APU generator.

9. The GTCP APU ignition is controlled by the APU control unit. It begins ignition at _____ % rpm and automatically turns it off at _____ % rpm.

Questions 10–19 refer to the Lycoming T53 turboshaft engine.

10. The T53-L-13B engine is a _____ -turbine engine designed primarily for _____ applications.

11. The T53-L-13B has a _____ -stage axial-flow _____ -stage centrifugal compressor, a _____ -stage gas-producer turbine, and a _____ -stage power turbine.

12. The gas-producer turbine rotors drive the _____ rotor, and, coaxial with it, the power-turbine rotors drive the _____ shaft.

13. Three sets of vanes in the air diffuser convert the air velocity into _____ and redirect the airflow rearward to the _____ .

14. As the air enters the combustion area, its flow direction is _____ .

15. Hot scavenge oil, draining through the lower strut into the accessory drive gearbox, anti-ices the bottom of the _____ area.

16. The interstage bleed system is supplied with the engine to improve _____ acceleration characteristics.

17. The interstage bleed system automatically relieves the compressor of a small amount of air to prevent compressor stall in the low-speed range and during compressor _____ or _____ .

18. The torquemeter is a hydromechanical torque-measuring device located in the _____ section of the engine inlet housing.

19. The torquemeter uses engine oil as the means for determining and measuring engine torque, which is read in the cockpit as psi _____ pressure.

Questions 20–29 refer to the Allison 250-C20 engine.

20. The Allison 250-C20 engine is composed of four major sections, or modules. These are the _____ section, the _____ section, the _____ section, and the _____ section.

21. The compressor is at the _____ of the engine, the combustion chamber is at the _____ , and the turbine section is near the _____ .

22. The turbine consists of a _____ -stage gas-producer rotor and a _____ -stage power-turbine rotor.

23. The power turbine drives the output shaft through the _____ train.

24. A two-stage helical and spur-gear set is used to reduce the rotational speed from 33,290 rpm at the power turbine to _____ rpm at the output drive spline.

25. The lubrication system for the Allison 250-C20 turbine engine is a _____ -sump system.

26. In the drive coupling between the engine and the transmission is a _____ clutch, which allows the rotor systems to continue to operate even if the engine stops.

27. "Split needles" describes a condition in which the percentage of N_R is greater than the percentage of N_2; when the needles are split, the engine delivers _____ power to the helicopter rotor and the helicopter rotor delivers _____ power to the engine.

28. Helicopters powered by the 250-C20 engine do not incorporate a clutch system because the _____-turbine design permits the starter to crank the gas-producer system without any helicopter rotor load on the starter.

29. _____ is a condition of flight in which the helicopter rotor (N_R) speed and the resultant lift are derived entirely from the airflow up through the rotor system.

Chapter 17

Name _____

Date _____

APPLICATION QUESTIONS

1. List the various models of the Allison 250 turboshaft engine.

   a. _____

   b. _____

   c. _____

   d. _____

2. What are the components of the Allison 250 fuel system?

   a. _____

   b. _____

   c. _____

   d. _____

3. What is a turboshaft engine primarily designed to produce?

   _____

4. What does a torquemeter use for determining and measuring torque? _____

Chapter 17

Name _____

Date _____

REVIEW EXAM

1. How many fuel nozzles does the Allison 250 turbine engine have?
   a. 3
   b. 1
   c. 14
   d. 4

2. How many gas-producer turbine stages are there?
   a. 1
   b. 2
   c. 4
   d. 6

3. The power turbine drives the compressor.
   a. True
   b. False

4. The Allison 250 uses a wet-sump lubrication system.
   a. True
   b. False

5. Which of the following components is not directly powered by the gas-producer turbine?
   a. Compressor
   b. Gas-producer fuel control
   c. Power-turbine governor
   d. Fuel pump

6. How many series of the model 250 have been commercially produced?
   a. 4
   b. 5
   c. 6
   d. 7

7. The Allison model 250 can be broken down into how many basic modules?
   a. 3
   b. 4
   c. 5
   d. 6

8. The compressor section of the model 250-C20 utilizes how many axial stages?
   a. 6
   b. 5
   c. 3
   d. 4

9. The Allison 250 engine uses the reversing airflow method.
   a. True
   b. False

10. The power turbine drives the compressor.
    a. True
    b. False

11. In the Allison 250-C20, what mechanically connects the gas-producer turbine and the power turbine together?
    a. Shaft
    b. Gears
    c. Nothing
    d. None of the above

12. The Allison 250-C20 turbine engine has
    a. a single-stage, dual-entry centrifugal compressor.
    b. a dual-stage, dual-entry centrifugal compressor.
    c. a single-stage, single-entry centrifugal compressor.
    d. an axial-flow compressor and a centrifugal-flow compressor.

Chapter 18

STUDY QUESTIONS

1. The engine pod or nacelle should be checked for loose material, tools, and other items which could be ingested by the engine and cause _____ damage to vanes, blades, and other interior parts.

2. For starting purposes, small gas-turbine engines are often equipped with starter- _____ .

3. Large gas-turbine engines are generally equipped with _____ starters.

4. If, during the starting of a gas-turbine engine, the EGT exceeds the prescribed safe limit, the engine is said to have had a _____ start.

5. If the engine fails to accelerate properly or does not reach the idle RPM position, the starting attempt is called a _____ start, or a _____ start.

6. A _____ cycle is normally defined as one takeoff and landing.

7. Inspections that are required after a given number of operation hours, flight cycles, or a combination of both are called _____ inspections.

8. Among some of the events which may cause the engine to require _____ inspections are foreign-object ingestion, bird ingestion, ice ingestion, overlimit operation (temperature and rpm), excessive "G" loads, and any other event that could cause internal or external engine damage.

9. A variation on the rigid borescope that is also used for examining the interiors of engines is the flexible _____ .

10. _____ damage to a gas-turbine engine may consist of anything from small nicks and scratches to complete disablement or destruction of the engine.

11. Fan blade shingling is the _____ of the midspan shrouds of the fan blades.

12. At starting, the most critical parameter for the engine is _____ .

13. Overspeed inspection of a typical high-bypass fan engine is primarily concerned with _____ assemblies.

14. A _____ inspection is needed to determine the integrity of the components in the hot section of the engine.

15. Hot section inspections generally are performed on either a _____ basis or an _____ basis.

16. _____ refers to both the work that is required to maintain an engine and its systems in an airworthy condition while it is installed in an aircraft and the work that is required to return an engine to airworthy condition once it has been removed from an aircraft.

17. _____ maintenance includes the periodic and recurring inspections that must be made in accordance with the engine section of the aircraft maintenance schedule.

18. _____ maintenance includes work necessitated by occurrences that are not normally related to time limits, such as bird ingestion, a strike by lightning, or heavy landing.

19. The scope of _____ maintenance includes removal and installation of external components, engine accessories, and hot section inspection.

20. Before an inspection of the air intake or exhaust system is begun, it must be ascertained that there is absolutely no possibility of the _____ system being operated.

21. PT6A fuel nozzles are subjected to two separate tests, the _____ test and the _____ test.

22. The purpose of the PT6A functional test is to observe the correct spray _____ .

23. As an engine operates, deposits accumulate on the engine's internal gas path to the point of deteriorating the engine's performance. To recover this performance loss, a _____ must be performed.

24. In the past, most engines were allowed a specified number of hours of operation before they needed to be overhauled. This period became known as the _____ .

25. Many engines have proven to be so reliable that they are overhauled only when they need major maintenance. This concept is referred to as _____ maintenance or overhaul.

26. Because of the high rotational speeds, any unbalance in the main _____ assembly of a gas-turbine engine is capable of producing vibrations and stresses which increase as the square of the rotational speed.

27. The _____ check may be required during or after inspection or maintenance to ensure that the engine rotates freely, that instrumentation functions properly, and that starter operation meets speed requirements for successful starts.

28. When it is necessary to check the operation of fuel-system components after removal and replacement or to perform a depreservation of the fuel system, the _____ check is employed.

29. The _____ check is performed to make sure that the engine will achieve takeoff power on a hot day without exceeding rpm and temperature limitations.

30. The process of adjusting the fuel control unit so that the engine will produce its rated thrust at the designated rpm is referred to as _____ the engine.

31. _____ may be defined as the detection of fault indications and the isolation of the fault or faults causing the indications.

32. _____ indicators include any instruments or devices on an aircraft which can give a member of the crew information about a developing problem in the operation of the engine.

33. The recording and analysis of gas-turbine engine performance and certain mechanical parameters over a period of time is called _____ .

Chapter 18

APPLICATION QUESTIONS

1. Define the term "foreign-object damage."

   _____

   _____

2. The basic requirements for starting a gas-turbine engine are

   a. _____

   b. _____

   c. _____

3. What is the safe distance from the intake of a gas-turbine engine while it is operating? _____

4. If the EGT exceeds the prescribed safe limit during the starting of a gas-turbine engine, what is the starting attempt called? _____

5. If a gas-turbine engine fails to accelerate properly, or does not reach idle, what is the starting attempt called?

   _____

6. What causes a false or hung start?

   _____

7. What type of starter is generally used on large gas-turbine engines? _____

8. List six steps that must be performed during an "A" check.

   a. _____

   b. _____

   c. _____

   d. _____

   e. _____

   f. _____

9. List the three types of scopes used for inspection of the interior of a gas-turbine engine.

   a. _____

   b. _____

   c. _____

10. Define the term "continuous maintenance" as it pertains to gas-turbine engines.

    _____

    _____

11. List the engine parameters that are used to measure and evaluate engine performance during testing.

a. _____

b. _____

c. _____

d. _____

e. _____

f. _____

g. _____

h. _____

i. _____

j. _____

12. Calculate the delta correction factor if the barometric pressure is 30.13 inHg. _____

13. Calculate the correction factor for theta, where the temperature is 24°C. _____

14. What is the corrected N_2 if the observed N_2 is 92% and the temperature is 23°C? _____

15. What is the corrected fuel flow if the observed fuel flow is 430 lb/h, the barometric pressure is 30.01 inHg, and the temperature is 26°C? _____

16. What is the purpose of a power assurance check?

_____

_____

17. What is the purpose of conditioned monitoring?

_____

_____

_____

Chapter 18

REVIEW EXAM

1. The blending of blades and vanes in a turbine engine
   a. is usually done only at engine overhaul.
   b. should be performed parallel to the length of the blade using smooth contours to minimize stress points.
   c. should be performed perpendicular to the length of the blade using smooth contours to minimize stress points.
   d. may sometimes be done with the engine installed, ordinarily using power tools.

2. During starting of a turbine engine,
   a. a hot start is indicated if the exhaust-gas temperature exceeds specified limits.
   b. an excessively lean mixture is likely to cause a hot start.
   c. the engine should start from 60 to 80 s after the fuel shutoff lever is opened.
   d. the starter switch should be released as soon as lightoff is indicated.

3. During starting of a turbine engine, a hung start is indicated if
   a. exhaust-gas temperature exceeds specified limits.
   b. the engine fails to reach idle rpm.
   c. engine rpm exceeds specified operating speed.
   d. engine pressure ratio exceeds specified operating limits.

4. What must the technician do after replacing the fuel control unit on a turbine engine?
   a. Retime the engine
   b. Recalibrate the fuel nozzles
   c. Retrim the engine
   d. Recheck the flame pattern

5. What is the first instrument indication of a successful start of a turbine engine?
   a. A decrease in the exhaust-gas temperature
   b. A rise in the engine fuel flow
   c. A decrease in the engine pressure ratio
   d. A rise in the exhaust-gas temperature

6. Who establishes the recommended operating time between overhauls (TBO) for a turbine engine used in general aviation?
   a. The engine manufacturer
   b. The operator working in conjunction with the FAA
   c. The owner/operator
   d. The FAA

7. Consider the following statements.
   (1) Gas welding and straightening of turbine-engine rotating airfoils does not require special equipment.
   (2) Gas welding and straightening of turbine-engine rotating airfoils is quite often recommended by the manufacturer.
   Of these two statements,

   a. only No. 1 is true.
   b. only No. 2 is true.
   c. both No. 1 and No. 2 are true.
   d. neither No. 1 nor No. 2 is true.

8. A type of repair of turbine-engine compressor blade coded areas is accomplished by a procedure termed "blending." Consider the following statements.
   (1) Blending is a hand method of recontouring damaged blades and vanes.
   (2) Blending requires the use of small files, emery cloth, and honing stones.
   Of these two statements,

   a. only No. 1 is true.
   b. only No. 2 is true.
   c. both No. 1 and No. 2 are true.
   d. neither No. 1 nor No. 2 is true.

9. Who establishes the recommended operating time between overhauls (TBO) for a turbine engine used in air carrier operation?
   a. The engine manufacturer
   b. The operator working in conjunction with the FAA
   c. The owner/operator
   d. The FAA

10. Who establishes mandatory replacement times for critical components of turbine engines?
    a. The owner/operator
    b. The FAA
    c. The operator working in conjunction with the FAA
    d. The engine manufacturer

11. Where do stress-rupture cracks usually appear on the turbine blades of turbojet engines?
    a. Across the blade root, parallel to the fir tree
    b. Along the trailing edge, parallel to the edge
    c. Along the leading edge, parallel to the edge
    d. Across the leading or trailing edge at a right angle to the edge length

12. When the leading edge of a first-stage turbine blade is found to have stress-rupture cracks, which of the following should be suspected?
    a. Air-seal wear
    b. Faulty cooling shield
    c. Overtemperature condition
    d. Overspeed condition

13. Damage to turbine vanes is apt to be greater than damage to compressor vanes because turbine vanes are subjected to much greater
    a. stress in the combustor.
    b. heat stress.
    c. thrust clearance.
    d. vibrations and other stresses.

14. Each jet engine turbine blade removed for detailed inspection must be reinstalled in
    a. a slot 180° away.
    b. a slot 90° clockwise.
    c. a slot 90° counterclockwise.
    d. the same slot.

15. When aircraft turbine blades are subjected to excessive temperatures, what type of failures can be expected?
    a. Compression and torsion
    b. Bending and torsion
    c. Torsion and tension
    d. Stress-rupture

16. Compressor field cleaning on turbine engines is performed primarily in order to
    a. prevent engine oil contamination and subsequent engine bearing wear or damage.
    b. facilitate flight line inspection of engine inlet and compressor areas for defects or FOD.
    c. obtain accurate spectrometric oil analysis readings.
    d. prevent engine performance degradation, increased fuel costs, and damage or corrosion to gas-path surfaces.

17. What is the proper starting sequence for a turbojet engine?
    a. Ignition, starter, fuel
    b. Fuel, starter, ignition
    c. Starter, ignition, fuel
    d. Starter, fuel, ignition

18. During starting of a turbojet engine, the starter should be disengaged
    a. when the engine lights are off.
    b. after the engine has reached self-accelerating speed.
    c. only after the engine has reached full idle rpm.
    d. when the ignition and fuel system are activated.

19. The procedure for removing accumulated dirt deposits from compressor blades is called
    a. the soak method.
    b. field cleaning.
    c. the purging process.
    d. reversed cleaning.

20. Which of the following is used to accomplish internal inspection of installed turbine engines?
    (1) Infrared photography
    (2) Ultrasound
    (3) A borescope
    (4) Fluorescent penetrant and ultraviolet light

    a. 1, 2, 3
    b. 1, 3
    c. 3
    d. 4

21. Which of the following is *not* a factor in the operation of an automatic fuel control unit on a turbojet engine?
    a. Compressor inlet-air density
    b. Compressor rpm
    c. Mixture control position
    d. Throttle position

22. A turbine-engine hot section is particularly susceptible to which of the following kinds of damage?
    a. Scoring
    b. Pitting
    c. Cracking
    d. Galling

23. Severe rubbing of turbine-engine compressor blades will usually cause
    a. bowing.
    b. cracking.
    c. burning.
    d. galling.

24. If a turbine engine is unable to reach takeoff EPR before its EGT limit is reached, this is an indication that
    a. the fuel control must be replaced.
    b. the EGT controller is out of adjustment.
    c. the ambient temperature is above 100° F.
    d. the compressor may be contaminated or damaged.

25. Why does a turbine engine require a cool-off period before being shut down?
    a. To allow the surfaces contacted by the lubricating oil to return to normal operating temperature
    b. To burn off excess fuel ahead of the fuel control
    c. To allow the turbine wheel to cool before the case contracts around it
    d. To avoid seizure of the engine bearings

26. Removal of a turbojet engine for maintenance or test-cell operation should be performed
    a. under the supervision of FAA personnel.
    b. in accordance with the manufacturer's instructions.
    c. by the aircraft owner or operator.
    d. by any FAA certificated repair station.

27. Consider the following statements.
    (1) Accumulation of contaminants in the compressor of a turbojet engine reduces aerodynamic efficiency of the blades.
    (2) Two common methods for removing dirt deposits from turbojet-engine compressor blades are fluid washing and abrasive grit blasting.
    Of these two statements,

    a. only No. 1 is true.
    b. only No. 2 is true.
    c. both No. 1 and No. 2 are true.
    d. neither No. 1 nor No. 2 is true.

28. Which of the following can cause fan-blade shingling in a turbofan engine?
    (1) Engine overspeed
    (2) Engine overtemperature
    (3) Large, rapid throttle movements
    (4) FOD

    a. 1
    b. 1, 2
    c. 1, 2, 3, 4
    d. 1, 4

29. Which of the following is used to monitor the mechanical integrity of the turbines, as well as to check engine operating conditions, of a turbojet engine?
    a. Engine oil pressure
    b. Exhaust-gas temperature
    c. Engine oil temperature
    d. Engine pressure ratio

30. Consider the following statements.
    (1) Serviceability limits for turbine blades are much more stringent than are those for turbine nozzle vanes.
    (2) A limited number of small nicks and dents can usually be permitted in any area of a turbine blade.
    Of these two statements,

    a. both No. 1 and No. 2 are true.
    b. neither No. 1 nor No. 2 is true.
    c. only No. 1 is true.
    d. only No. 2 is true.

31. Which of the following conditions is usually not acceptable to any extent in turbine blades?
    a. Cracks
    b. Nicks
    c. Pits
    d. Dents

32. What instrument on a gas-turbine engine should be monitored to minimize the possibility of a "hot" start?
    a. rpm indicator
    b. Turbine inlet temperature gage
    c. Horsepower meter
    d. Torquemeter

33. For what primary purpose is a turbine-engine fuel control unit trimmed?
    a. To obtain new exhaust-gas temperature limits
    b. To obtain maximum thrust output when desired
    c. To properly position the power levers
    d. To adjust the idle rpm

34. Under which of the following conditions will trimming of a turbine engine be most accurate?
    a. Low moisture and a tail wind
    b. High wind and high moisture
    c. High moisture and low wind
    d. No wind and low moisture

35. For trimming of a turbine engine, the fuel control is adjusted to
    a. produce as much power as the engine is capable of producing.
    b. limit idle rpm and maximum speed or EPR.
    c. allow the engine to produce maximum rpm without regard to power output.
    d. restrict power to 100% without regard to specified rpm.

Chapter 19

1. Each blade of an aircraft propeller is essentially a _____ wing.

2. As a result of their construction, propeller blades produce forces that create _____ to pull or push the airplane through the air.

3. On low-horsepower engines, the propeller is mounted on a shaft that is usually an extension of the _____ .

4. On high-horsepower engines, the propeller is mounted on a propeller shaft that is _____ to the engine crankshaft.

5. The first satisfactory theory for the design of aircraft propellers was known as the _____ theory. This theory was evolved in 1909 by a Polish scientist named Dryewiecki; therefore, it is sometimes referred to as the _____ theory.

6. According to the blade-element theory, each element must be designed as part of the blade to operate at its own best _____ to create thrust when revolving at its best design speed.

7. The thrust developed by a propeller is in accordance with Newton's _____ law of motion.

8. A _____ -pitch propeller is one that makes use of the blade-element theory.

9. Blade _____ are designated distances measured in inches along the blade as measured from the center of the hub.

10. The angle between the face or chord of a particular blade section and the plane in which the propeller blades rotate is called the _____ angle.

11. The gradual change of blade section angles is called _____ distribution.

12. The angle of attack of a propeller blade section is the angle between the face of the blade section and the direction of the _____ wind.

13. The actual distance the airplane moves forward during one revolution (360°) of the propeller in flight is called the _____ pitch.

14. The _____ pitch is the distance an element of the propeller would advance in one revolution if it were moving along a helix having an angle equal to its blade angle.

15. The difference between the geometrical pitch and the effective pitch of a propeller is defined as _____ .

16. The slip function is the ratio of the speed of advance through undisturbed air to the product of the propeller _____ and the number of revolutions per unit time.

17. The _____ pitch, also called the experimental mean pitch, is the distance a propeller would have to advance in one revolution to give no thrust.

18. The component of the total air force on the propeller which is parallel to the direction of advance is called _____ .

19. _____ force is a physical force that tends to throw the rotating propeller blades away from the hub.

20. Torque bending force is the form of air resistance that tends to bend the propeller blades in a direction that is _____ to the direction of rotation.

21. _____ bending force is the thrust load that tends to bend propeller blades forward as the aircraft is pulled through the air.

22. Aerodynamic twisting force tends to turn the blades to a _____ blade angle.

23. Centrifugal twisting force tends to force the blades toward a _____ blade angle.

24. The _____ horsepower is the actual amount of horsepower that an engine-propeller unit transforms into thrust.

25. The ratio of the thrust horsepower to the torque horsepower is the _____ of the propeller.

26. The tips of the propeller blades must have at least _____ inches of radial clearance from the fuselage or any other part of the aircraft structure.

27. Propellers mounted on the front end of the engine structure are called _____ propellers.

28. _____ propellers are propellers mounted on the rear end of the engine behind the supporting structure.

29. A _____ -pitch propeller is a rigidly constructed propeller on which the blade angles may not be altered without bending or reworking the blades.

30. The pitch setting of a _____ -adjustable propeller can be adjusted only with tools on the ground, when the engine is not operating.

31. A _____ -pitch propeller is one provided with a means of control for adjusting the angle of the blades during flight.

32. With automatic-pitch propellers, the blade-angle change within a preset range occurs automatically as a result of _____ forces acting on the blades.

33. The constant-speed propeller utilizes a hydraulically or electrically operated pitch-changing mechanism controlled by a _____ .

34. The term _____ refers to the operation of rotating the blades of a propeller to an edge-to-the-wind position for the purpose of stopping the rotation of the propeller.

35. If a propeller is not feathered when its engine stops driving it, the propeller will _____ and cause excessive drag, which could be detrimental to aircraft operation.

36. A reverse-pitch propeller is a constant speed propeller for which the blade angles can be changed to a _____ value during operation.

37. A reverse-pitch propeller is used principally as an _____ brake to reduce ground roll after landing.

38. A fixed-pitch metal propeller is usually manufactured by forging a single bar of _____ alloy to the required shape.

39. Some types of fixed forces that are used to move constant-speed propeller blades are _____ , _____ , _____ , and air/_____ charges.

40. The main variable force used to change blade angle is governor _____ pressure, which is metered by the speed-sensing section of the propeller governor.

41. The speed sensing in a propeller governor is accomplished by means of rotating _____ in the upper part of the governor body.

42. On the Hartzell nonfeathering steel-hub propeller, the counterweights attached to the blade clamps utilize centrifugal force to _____ the pitch of the blades.

43. Hartzell constant-speed, full-feathering steel-hub propellers utilize hydraulic pressure to _____ the pitch of the blades and a combination of spring and counterweight forces to _____ the pitch.

44. On the Hartzell compact (aluminum-hub) air pressure–counterweight–oil propellers, a combination of air pressure and blade counterweights is used to _____ pitch and _____ the propeller.

45. The Hamilton Standard Hydromatic Propeller uses centrifugal twisting moment to turn the blades to a _____ angle. The high-pressure _____ is directed to the propeller to change the blade angle in either direction.

46. Propeller anti-icing may be accomplished by spraying _____ along the leading edges of the blades.

47. A deicing system which is extensively used is heating of the blades by _____ heating elements.

48. Controlling the propellers so that they operate at the same speed is called _____ .

49. Controlling the propeller-blade phase angle as well as the speed is called _____ .

Chapter 19

Name _____

Date _____

APPLICATION QUESTIONS

1. Define "blade angle."

   _____

   _____

2. Define "blade stations."

   _____

   _____

3. By means of a simple sketch, show the relationship among geometric pitch, effective pitch, and slip.

4. Calculate the geometric pitch of a propeller if it has an angle of 20° at the 30-in blade station.

   _____

5. List the five forces acting on a propeller in flight.

   a. _____

   b. _____

   c. _____

   d. _____

   e. _____

6. List the following propeller clearances.

   a. Ground clearances

   _____

   b. Water clearance

   _____

   c. Structural clearances

   _____

7. List the two general classifications of propellers.

   a. _____

   b. _____

8. List the types of propellers.

a. _____

b. _____

c. _____

d. _____

e. _____

f. _____

9. Describe propeller feathering.

_____

_____

10. Why is propeller feathering necessary?

_____

_____

_____

11. List the three positions of a propeller governor.

a. _____

b. _____

c. _____

12. List the types of fixed forces that are used to move propeller blades.

a. _____

b. _____

c. _____

d. _____

13. What is the main variable force used to change propeller blade angle? _____

14. If the governor flyweights are tilted out, what position does this put the governor in? _____

15. If the speeder-spring force and the flyweight force are in equilibrium, what governor position is this?

_____

16. What position is the governor in if the flyweights are tilted in? _____

17. What two types of systems are used to eliminate or prevent icing from occurring on the propellers?

a. _____

b. _____

18. Describe the basic function of a synchrophasing system.

_____

_____

_____

Chapter 19

Name _____

Date _____

REVIEW EXAM

1. How is aircraft electrical power for the propeller deicer system transferred from the engine to the propeller hub assembly?
   a. By slip rings and segment plates
   b. By slip rings and brushes
   c. By collector ring and transducer
   d. By flexible electrical connectors

2. How is anti-icing fluid ejected from the slinger ring on a propeller?
   a. By ejector valves
   b. By pump pressure
   c. By centripetal force
   d. By centrifugal force

3. On most reciprocating multiengine aircraft, automatic propeller synchronization is accomplished through actuation of the
   a. blade switches.
   b. throttle levers.
   c. propeller governors.
   d. propeller control levers.

4. Propeller fluid anti-icing systems generally use which of the following?
   a. Ethylene glycol
   b. Isopropyl alcohol
   c. Denatured alcohol
   d. Ethyl alcohol

5. What is a function of the automatic propeller synchronizing system on multiengine aircraft?
   a. To increase vibration and reduce noise
   b. To control the tip speed of all propellers
   c. To control engine rpm and reduce vibration
   d. To control the power output of all engines

6. Ice formation on propellers, when the aircraft is in flight, will
   a. decrease thrust and cause excessive vibration.
   b. increase aircraft stall speed and increase noise.
   c. decrease aircraft stall speed and increase noise.
   d. increase thrust and cause excessive vibration.

7. What unit in the propeller anti-icing system controls the output of the pump?
   a. Pressure relief valve
   b. Rheostat
   c. Cycling timer
   d. Current limiter

8. Proper operation of electric deicing boots on individual propeller blades may best be determined by
   a. feeling the boots to determine if they are hot.
   b. observing the ammeter or loadmeter for current flow.
   c. timing the inflation and deflation sequence.
   d. checking the ammeter for flickering and feeling the boots for sequence of heating.

9. A propeller synchrophasing system allows a pilot to reduce noise and vibration by
   a. adjusting the phase angle between the propellers.
   b. varying the speeds of all propellers.
   c. adjusting the planes of rotation of all propellers.
   d. setting the pitch angles of all propellers exactly the same.

10. A powerplant using a hydraulically controlled constant-speed propeller is operating within the propeller's constant speed range at a fixed throttle setting. If the tension of the propeller governor control spring (speeder spring) is reduced by movement of the cockpit propeller control,
    a. the propeller blade angle will increase, engine manifold pressure will increase, and engine rpm will decrease.
    b. the propeller blade angle will decrease, engine manifold pressure will increase, and engine rpm will decrease.
    c. the propeller blade angle will decrease, engine manifold pressure will decrease, and engine rpm will increase.
    d. the propeller blade angle will increase, engine manifold pressure will decrease, and engine rpm will increase.

11. During engine operation at speeds lower than those for which the constant-speed propeller control can govern in the INCREASE RPM position, the propeller will
    a. remain in the full LOW RPM position.
    b. remain in the full HIGH PITCH position.
    c. maintain engine rpm in the normal manner until the HIGH PITCH stop is reached.
    d. remain in the full LOW PITCH position.

12. The propeller governor
    a. controls the flow of oil to and from the pitch-change mechanism.
    b. controls the relief valve in the accumulator assembly.
    c. controls the spring tension on the boost pump speeder spring.
    d. prevents the linkage and counterweights from moving in and out.

13. When a propeller is in the on-speed condition,
    a. the centrifugal force acting on the governor flyweights is greater than the tension of the speeder spring.
    b. the tension of the speeder spring is greater than the centrifugal force acting on the governor flyweights.
    c. the tension of the speeder spring is less than the centrifugal force acting on the governor flyweights.
    d. the centrifugal force of the governor flyweights is equal to the speeder-spring force.

14. What actuates the pilot valve in the governor of a constant-speed propeller?
    a. Engine oil pressure
    b. Governor flyweights
    c. Propeller control lever
    d. Governor pump oil pressure

15. What will happen to the propeller blade angle and the engine rpm if the tension on the propeller governor control spring (speeder spring) is increased?
    a. Blade angle will increase and rpm will increase.
    b. Blade angle will decrease and rpm will decrease.
    c. Blade angle will increase and rpm will decrease.
    d. Blade angle will decrease and rpm will increase.

16. When the centrifugal force acting on the propeller governor counterweights overcomes the tension of the speeder spring, a propeller is in what speed condition?
    a. On-speed condition
    b. Underspeed condition
    c. In-between condition
    d. Overspeed condition

17. What operational force causes the greatest stress on a propeller?
    a. Aerodynamic twisting force
    b. Centrifugal force
    c. Thrust bending force
    d. Torque bending force

18. What operational force tends to increase propeller blade angle?
    a. Centrifugal twisting force
    b. Aerodynamic twisting force
    c. Thrust bending force
    d. Torque bending force

19. Which of the following functions requires the use of a propeller blade station?
    a. Blade angle measurement
    b. Propeller installation and removal
    c. Blade indexing
    d. Propeller balancing

20. During which of the following conditions of flight will the blade pitch angle of a constant-speed propeller be the greatest?
    a. Approach to landing
    b. Climb following takeoff
    c. High-speed, high-altitude cruising flight
    d. Takeoff from sea level

21. The actual distance a propeller moves forward through the air during one revolution is known as the
    a. effective pitch.
    b. geometric pitch.
    c. relative pitch.
    d. resultant pitch.

22. Which of the following is a true statement regarding movement of the throttle on a reciprocating engine when the propeller is in the constant-speed range and the engine is developing cruise power?
    a. Opening the throttle will cause an increase in blade angle.
    b. Closing the throttle will cause an increase in blade angle.
    c. The rpm will vary directly with any movement of the throttle.
    d. Movement of the throttle will not affect the blade angle.

23. Propeller blade stations are measured from the
    a. index mark on the blade shank.
    b. hub centerline.
    c. blade base.
    d. blade tip.

24. The thrust produced by a rotating propeller is a result of
    a. propeller slippage.
    b. an area of low pressure behind the propeller blades.
    c. an area of decreased pressure immediately in front of the propeller blades.
    d. the angle of relative wind and rotational velocity of the propeller.

25. The angle of attack of a rotating propeller blade is measured between the blade chord or face and which of the following?
    a. Plane of blade rotation
    b. Full low-pitch blade angle
    c. Relative airstream
    d. Geometric pitch angle required to produce the same thrust

26. The centrifugal twisting moment (CTM) of an operating propeller tends to
    a. increase the pitch angle.
    b. reduce the pitch angle.
    c. bend the blades in the direction of rotation.
    d. bend the blades rearward in the line of flight.

27. Which of the following is identified as the cambered or curved side of a propeller blade, corresponding to the upper surface of a wing airfoil section?
    a. Blade back
    b. Blade chord
    c. Blade leading edge
    d. Blade face

28. Which of the following best describes the blade movement of a full-feathering, constant-speed propeller that is in the LOW RPM position when the feathering action is begun?
    a. High pitch through low pitch to feather position
    b. Low pitch directly to feather position
    c. High pitch directly to feather position
    d. Low pitch through high pitch to feather position

29. What is the primary purpose of the metal tipping which covers the blade tips and extends along the leading edge of each wood propeller blade?
    a. To increase the lateral strength of the blade
    b. To prevent impact damage to the tip and leading edge of the blade
    c. To increase the longitudinal strength of the blade
    d. To provide a true airfoil along the entire length of the blade

30. Blade angle is an angle formed by a line perpendicular to the crankshaft and a line formed by the
    a. relative wind.
    b. apparent wind.
    c. chord of the blade.
    d. blade face.

31. The aerodynamic force acting on a rotating propeller blade operating at a normal pitch angle tends to
    a. reduce the pitch angle.
    b. increase the pitch angle.
    c. bend the blades rearward in the line of flight.
    d. bend the blades in the direction of rotation.

32. Which of the following forces or combination of forces operates to move the blades of a constant-speed counterweight-type propeller to the HIGH PITCH position?
    a. Engine oil pressure acting on the propeller piston-cylinder arrangement
    b. Engine oil pressure acting on the propeller piston-cylinder arrangement and centrifugal force acting on the counterweights
    c. Centrifugal force acting on the counterweights
    d. Prop governor oil pressure acting on the propeller piston-cylinder arrangement

33. What controls the constant-speed range of a constant-speed propeller?
    a. Engine rpm
    b. Angle of climb and descent with accompanying changes in airspeed
    c. Number of blades
    d. The mechanical limits in the propeller pitch range

34. For takeoff, a constant-speed propeller is normally set in the
    a. HIGH PITCH, HIGH RPM position.
    b. LOW PITCH, LOW RPM position.
    c. HIGH PITCH, LOW RPM position.
    d. LOW PITCH, HIGH RPM position.

35. The primary purpose of a propeller is to
   a. create lift on the fixed airfoils of an aircraft.
   b. build up enough slipstream to support the airfoils.
   c. convert engine horsepower to thrust.
   d. provide static and dynamic stability of an aircraft in flight.

36. A constant-speed propeller provides maximum efficiency by
   a. increasing blade pitch as the aircraft speed decreases.
   b. adjusting blade angle for most conditions encountered in flight.
   c. reducing turbulence near the blade tips.
   d. increasing the lift coefficient of the blade.

37. The centrifugal twisting force acting on a propeller blade is
   a. greater than the aerodynamic twisting force and tends to move the blade to a higher angle.
   b. less than the aerodynamic twisting force and tends to move the blade to a lower angle.
   c. less than the aerodynamic twisting force and tends to move the blade to a higher angle.
   d. greater than the aerodynamic twisting force and tends to move the blade to a lower angle.

38. The geometric pitch of a propeller is defined as
   a. effective pitch minus slippage.
   b. effective pitch plus slippage.
   c. the angle between the blade chord and the plane of rotation.
   d. the angle between the blade face and the plane of rotation.

39. What operational force causes propeller blade tips to lag in the direction opposite to the direction of rotation?
   a. Thrust bending force
   b. Aerodynamic twisting force
   c. Centrifugal twisting force
   d. Torque bending force

40. What operational force tends to bend the propeller blades forward at the tip?
   a. Torque bending force
   b. Aerodynamic twisting force
   c. Centrifugal twisting force
   d. Thrust bending force

Chapter 20

STUDY QUESTIONS

1. When turboprops are discussed, brake horsepower is usually referred to as _____ horsepower, meaning the horsepower delivered to the propeller shaft.

2. With a turboprop engine, some jet velocity is left at the jet nozzle after the turbines have extracted the required energy for driving the compressor, reduction gear, accessories, etc. This velocity can be calculated as _____ .

3. When the shp and the net thrust are added together, the result is _____ horsepower.

Questions 4–8 refer to the Hartzell HC-B3TN turbopropeller system.

4. The piston is connected to the blade shanks by means of link arms, thus producing _____ of the blades as the piston moves.

5. There are three coaxial springs inside the piston-cylinder assembly. These constitute the _____ spring assembly.

6. When the piston moves forward and the pitch is _____ , the springs are compressed.

7. When the governor allows engine oil to flow from the propeller back to the engine, the springs and the force produced by the blade counterweights pull the piston back toward the hub and the blade pitch _____ .

8. The reversible propellers are provided with hydraulic low-pitch valves called _____ valves, which prevent the governor from moving the piston beyond a prescribed low-pitch position.

Questions 9–12 refer to the Dowty R321 four-blade turbopropeller.

9. The propeller blades are rotated to low-pitch and reverse pitch by means of _____ pressure. When the oil pressure is released, the blades rotate to high pitch and feathered positions by means of a combination of _____ and _____ forces.

10. Starting latches are incorporated in the cylinder to ensure that the propeller blades will remain in _____ pitch during engine starting.

11. The pitch-control mechanism is adjusted by means of two levers to select the operating mode for the propeller. The constant-speed governing mode is selected for _____ operations, and the beta mode is selected for _____ operations.

12. In case of engine failure, a _____ signal will be received by the torque sensor, which then moves to operate the feather valve hydraulically and feather the propeller.

13. The McCauley propeller is a single-acting unit in which hydraulic pressure moves the blades toward _____ pitch and springs and counterweights move the blades toward _____ pitch.

14. In comparison to the more traditional construction material (aluminum alloy), the material of the composite blade offers the following advantages.

   a. _____

   b. _____

   c. _____

   d. _____

   e. _____

15. In the construction of Dowty composite blades, two carbon fiber spars, separated by polyurethane foam, carry the main _____ and _____ loads, whereas a glass-and-carbon fiber shell provides _____ stiffness and forms the airfoil shape.

16. In the Dowty composite blades, _____ protection is provided by light alloy braiding laid into both faces of the blade.

Questions 17–29 refer to the PT6A reversing propeller installation.

17. The main _____ governor bleeds governor oil pressure from the propeller if an overspeed condition should occur.

18. The power-turbine governor has an air-bleed orifice that controls _____ flow to the gas generator.

19. The integrated engine and propeller combination has three cockpit controls: a _____ cutoff lever, a _____ control lever, and a _____ control lever.

20. The fuel cutoff lever usually has two positions: _____ and _____ .

21. When the control lever is moved to the MIN RPM position, the propeller will automatically _____ .

22. During low-airspeed operations, the propeller governor can be used to select the required blade _____ (beta control).

23. A propeller in low pitch _____ the load on the engine.

24. When the pilot valve plunger is centered, the propeller blade angle and engine speed remain _____ .

25. An _____ condition occurs as the result of an increase in propeller load or movement of the control lever in the INCREASE RPM direction.

26. An _____ condition occurs as the result of a decrease in propeller load or movement of the control lever in the DECREASE RPM direction.

27. Reverse pitch is obtained by moving the power lever aft of the _____ position.

28. Normally the air-bleed orifice will be opened at approximately _____ % above the propeller governor speed setting.

29. The solenoid-operated shutoff valve prevents the propeller from going into _____ pitch during normal flight operation.

Questions 30–36 refer to the Garrett TPE331 turbopropeller control system.

30. Governor oil pressure moves the propeller toward the _____ and _____ positions whereas a spring and counterweights move the propeller toward the _____ and _____ positions.

31. In the beta mode (ground operation), the underspeed governor controls _____ flow to the engine, thereby controlling _____ speed.

32. The _____ lever is mechanically connected to both the propeller pitch control and the main fuel control.

33. The function of the propeller pitch control in the beta mode is to meter the oil from the propeller governor pump into the propeller through the _____ tube.

34. If the oil pressure in the propeller piston is reduced, the propeller is moved toward the FEATHER position by _____ and _____ forces.

35. In the flight mode, the propeller governor controls _____ (set by the condition lever), and _____ is controlled by the fuel control through the power lever.

36. Because this system is a fixed-turbine type of engine, the propeller cannot be allowed to _____ on engine shutdown.

Questions 37–42 refer to the Allison 250-B17 reversing turbopropeller system.

37. The beta valve is considered to be the hydraulic _____ -pitch stop.

38. The condition lever has the capability of varying the propeller governor setting between _____ % and _____ % of propeller speed.

39. The function of the _____ is to provide automatic sequencing of the multiple powerplant controls in response to input from the pilot-operated power and condition levers.

40. During starting, propeller unfeathering will automatically occur, with the propeller _____ valve regulating the blade angle on completion of the start.

41. During taxi operation, the _____ lever should be in the MAXIMUM position. The _____ lever can be moved freely to obtain the desired thrust for taxiing.

42. During reverse-thrust operation, the _____ governor regulates the fuel flow and the _____ valve regulates the propeller blade angle.

Questions 43–44 refer to the General Electric CT7 propeller control system.

43. The propeller system operates in two modes: the _____ mode, for normal flight conditions; and the _____ control mode, for taxiing and reverse-thrust operations.

44. The power lever controls engine power output during the _____ mode and controls propeller blade pitch in the _____ control mode.

Chapter 20

Name _____

Date _____

APPLICATION QUESTIONS

1. State the formula for finding shaft horsepower on a turboprop propeller.

   _____

2. If a propeller is turning at 2000 rpm and developing 900 lb • ft of torque, what is the shaft horsepower?

   _____

3. If an aircraft is sitting static and is producing 680 shaft horsepower and is also producing 187.5 lb of thrust out the back, what is the equivalent shaft horsepower? _____

4. What is one advantage of a composite propeller blade over an aluminum-alloy blade?

   _____

5. What are the three cockpit controls for the PTA propeller control system?

   a. _____

   b. _____

   c. _____

6. What is the purpose of the solenoid-operated shutoff valve or lock-pitch solenoid valve?

   _____

7. In the PT6 propeller control system, what provides feedback to the beta valve when the amount of reverse called for is reached? _____

8. List the four controls or governors or valves that are used to make up the Garrett TPE331 engine turbopropeller control system.

   a. _____

   b. _____

   c. _____

   d. _____

Chapter 20

REVIEW EXAM

1. How is a propeller controlled in a large turboprop aircraft?
   a. Independently of the engine
   b. By varying the engine rpm except for feathering and reversing
   c. By varying the gear ratio between the propeller and the engine
   d. By the engine power lever

2. The Pratt & Whitney PT6A engine's overspeed governor controls prop rpm by
   a. venting P_y pressure.
   b. shutting off the flow of oil to the prop dome.
   c. bleeding (draining) oil from the prop back to the sump.
   d. none of these.

3. In the PT6A, the N_f (overspeed) governor will control prop rpm during the forward mode of operation at
   a. about 2332 rpm if prop control is set at 2000 rpm.
   b. 106% of 220 rpm.
   c. 106% of the current prop governor setting.
   d. 103% of the N.C.S. governor setting.

4. In flight on the PT6A engine, the pilot is prevented from pulling into reverse by
   a. the throttle switch.
   b. the nose and right gear squat switches only.
   c. the blade angle sensor switch (beta switch) only.
   d. the lock-pitch solenoid (shutoff) valve.

5. The purpose(s) of the lock-pitch solenoid (shutoff) valve on the PT6A is (are)
   a. to allow prop reversing in flight.
   b. to prevent prop reversing in flight.
   c. to feather the prop.
   d. all of the above.

6. Oil pressure moves a turbo propeller to
   a. REVERSE position.
   b. FEATHER position.
   c. LOW PITCH position.
   d. both REVERSE and LOW PITCH positions.

7. Counterweights and a spring are used to move a turbo propeller to
   a. REVERSE position.
   b. FEATHER position.
   c. LOW PITCH position.
   d. both FEATHER and LOW PITCH positions.

8. The beta ring provides
   a. feedback to the beta valve after prop travel.
   b. cam block adjustment.
   c. P_y bleed-line pressure.
   d. all of the above.

9. A turbo propeller system control lever, could be
   a. a throttle, prop. or mixture lever.
   b. a power, prop, or mixture lever.
   c. a power, prop, or condition lever.
   d. none of these.

10. What does the feathering valve do when it is moved to the FEATHER position in the TPE331 installation?
    a. Routes governor oil pressure to the propeller
    b. Routes air pressure to the propeller
    c. Stops all flow of oil, both to and from the propeller
    d. Releases oil from the propeller

Chapter 21

1. The integral-hub flange-type crankshaft is manufactured with the propeller mounting hub forged on the front end of the _____ .

2. _____ -type shafts are currently used on most opposed-type reciprocating engines.

3. When a fixed-pitch metal propeller is installed in the absence of dowel pins, the propeller should be positioned so that the blades are at the _____ o'clock and _____ o'clock positions when the engine is stopped.

4. Before a propeller is installed on a tapered shaft, the fit of the propeller on the shaft is checked by the use of _____ .

5. When a Hartzell compact flanged propeller is installed, the cylinder should be charged with _____ or _____ to the prescribed pressure.

6. If excessive gas pressure is used in charging a Hartzell compact hub, there is a possibility of _____ taking place at idle speed when the engine is warm and the oil is very thin.

7. When a McCauley flanged propeller is installed, it must be seated against the crankshaft flange with a straight push. Rotation, cocking, or wiggling of the propeller to seat it is likely to damage the O-ring groove, and _____ leakage may result.

8. When a new fixed-pitch propeller has been installed and operated, the hub bolts should always be inspected for tightness after the _____ and after _____ h of flying.

9. The purpose of propeller balancing is to reduce the _____ -per-rev vibration induced by the out-of-balance propeller.

10. The purpose of checking propeller track is to ensure that all blades of a propeller are flying in the same _____ of rotation.

11. A _____ alteration is an alteration which may cause an appreciable change in weight, balance, strength, performance, or other qualities affecting the airworthiness of a propeller.

12. A _____ alteration is any alteration not classified as a major alteration.

13. A _____ repair is any repair which may adversely affect any of the qualities noted in the definition of a major alteration.

14. A _____ repair is any repair other than a major repair.

15. Requirements governing persons or organizations authorized to perform maintenance and repairs on propellers are set forth in FAR Part _____ .

16. The inspection of steel blades may be either _____ or _____ .

17. A damaged metal propeller is one that has been _____ , _____ , or severely _____ .

18. Propeller blade failures usually occur because of _____ cracks, which start as mechanically formed dents, cuts, scars, scratches, nicks, or leading-edge pits.

19. Experience indicates that fatigue failures normally occur within a few inches of the blade _____ .

Questions 20–25 refer to composite propeller blades.

20. A separation of the metal erosion shield from the composite material in the blade is called a _____ .

21. _____ is an internal separation of the layers of a composite material.

22. An alteration of the original shape or size of a component is called a _____ .

23. A _____ is a small surface area where material has been removed by contact with a sharp object.

24. A delamination of the blade extending to the blade surface, normally found near the trailing edge or tip, is called a

_____ .

25. Composite propeller blades, unlike aluminum blades, are not subject to _____ cracks.

26. The blade angles of a propeller may be accurately checked by the use of a _____ .

27. The _____ rpm is checked during a power run-up to ensure that the engine is developing its rated power.

28. The static rpm is generally found in the aircraft's _____ .

29. On a _____ -pitch propeller, there is no means of adjusting the static rpm.

Chapter 21

Name _____

Date _____

APPLICATION QUESTIONS

1. List the three types of propeller hubs (crankshafts).

   a. _____

   b. _____

   c. _____

2. Explain how to correct front-cone bottoming.

   _____

   _____

   _____

3. Explain how to correct rear-cone bottoming.

   _____

   _____

   _____

4. Identify each item in the diagram below.

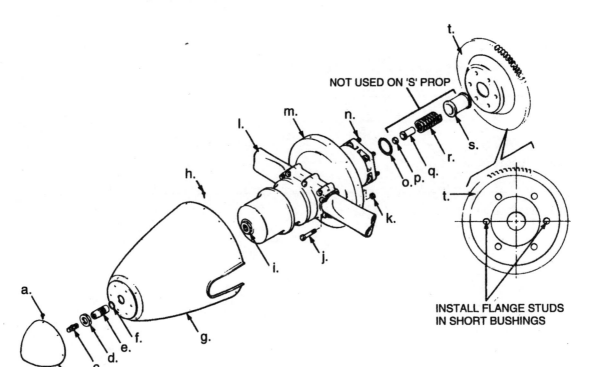

NOT USED ON 'S' PROP

INSTALL FLANGE STUDS
IN SHORT BUSHINGS

   a. _____

   b. _____

   c. _____

   d. _____

   e. _____

f. _____

g. _____

h. _____

i. _____

j. _____

k. _____

l. _____

m. _____

n. _____

o. _____

p. _____

q. _____

r. _____

s. _____

t. _____

5. What is the purpose of checking propeller track?

_____

6. What are the two positions at which a propeller should be checked during static balancing?

a. _____

b. _____

7. With regard to composite propeller blades, define "airworthy damage."

_____

_____

_____

8. What is the purpose of a coin-tap test?

_____

9. Why is the static rpm checked during a power run-up?

_____

Chapter 21

REVIEW EXAM

1. Which of the following would indicate a general weak-engine condition in an engine operated with a fixed-pitch propeller or test club?
   a. Oil pressure lower at idle rpm than at cruise rpm
   b. Lower-than-normal static rpm, full throttle operation
   c. Manifold pressure lower at idle rpm than at static rpm
   d. Lower-than-normal manifold pressure for any given rpm

2. A ground incident that results in sudden propeller stoppage may require a crankshaft runout inspection. What publication would be used to obtain crankshaft runout tolerance?
   a. Federal Aviation Regulations
   b. Current Manufacturer's Maintenance Manual or Instructions for Continued Airworthiness
   c. Type Certificate Data Sheet
   d. AC 43.13-1A, Acceptable Methods, Techniques and Practices—Aircraft Inspection and Repair

3. What type of imbalance will cause a two-blade propeller to have a persistent tendency to come to rest in a horizontal position (with the blades parallel to the ground) while being checked on a propeller balancing beam?
   a. Vertical
   b. Horizontal
   c. Dynamic
   d. Harmonic

4. What is the purpose of an arbor used in balancing a propeller?
   a. To support the propeller on the balance knives
   b. To level the balance stand
   c. To indicate the weight to be added or removed
   d. To mark the propeller blades where weights are to be attached

5. If a blade of a metal propeller is shortened because of damage to the tip, the remaining blade(s) must be
   a. ground down at the shank to balance the weight.
   b. reset (blade angle) to compensate for the shortened blade.
   c. returned to the manufacturer for alteration.
   d. reduced to conform with the shortened blade.

6. Which of the following is used to correct horizontal unbalance of a wood propeller?
   a. Putty
   b. Brass screws
   c. Shellac
   d. Solder

7. What determines the maximum amount which an aluminum-alloy propeller can be bent in face alignment and still be repairable by cold straightening?
   a. The thickness of the blade section in which the bend is located
   b. The chord length of the blade section in which the bend is located
   c. The linear distance from the blade tip to the location of the bend
   d. The linear distance from the propeller centerline to the location of the bend

8. The etching process is used during propeller overhaul to
   a. detect blade defects.
   b. identify unairworthy components.
   c. identify the blades.
   d. indicate the overhauling agency name and certificate number.

9. Why is it important that nicks in the leading edges of aluminum-alloy blades be removed as soon as possible?
   a. To localize vibratory stresses
   b. To maintain horizontal balance
   c. To improve the aerodynamic characteristics of the blades
   d. To eliminate a condition under which fatigue cracks can start

10. Major repairs of aluminum-alloy propellers and blades may be done by
    a. a powerplant mechanic working for a certificated A & P mechanic.
    b. any propeller manufacturer.
    c. an appropriately rated repair station or the manufacturer.
    d. a repairman, regardless of where he or she works.

11. In which of the following ways does front-cone bottoming occur during propeller installation?
    a. The front cone becomes bottomed in the front propeller hub cone seat before the rear propeller hub cone seat has engaged the rear cone.
    b. The front cone becomes bottomed in the front propeller hub cone seat before the retaining nut has engaged sufficient threads to be safetied properly.
    c. The front cone enters the front propeller hub cone seat at an angle, causing the propeller retaining nut to appear tight when it is only partially tightened.
    d. The front cone contacts the ends of the shaft splines, preventing the front and rear cones from being tightened against the cone in the propeller hub.

12. What is indicated when the front cone bottoms during installation of a propeller?
    a. The propeller retaining nut torque is correct.
    b. The propeller-dome combination is incorrect.
    c. The blade angles are incorrect.
    d. The rear cone should be moved forward.

13. The primary purpose of the front and rear cones for a propeller that is installed on a splined shaft is
    a. to position the propeller hub on the splined shaft.
    b. to prevent metal-to-metal contact between the propeller and the splined shaft.
    c. to reduce stresses between the splines of the propeller and the splines of the shaft.
    d. to balance the propeller aerodynamically.

14. Maximum taper contact between crankshaft and propeller hub is determined by using
    a. a telescoping gage.
    b. bearing blue color transfer.
    c. a micrometer.
    d. a surface gage.

15. Propeller blade tracking is the process of determining
    a. the plane of rotation of the propeller with respect to the aircraft longitudinal axis.
    b. that each blade has the same angle of attack, to prevent vibration.
    c. that the blade angles are within the specified tolerance of each other.
    d. the positions of the tips of the propeller blades relative to each other.

Chapter 22

1. Pressure instruments are usually of the _____ type, the _____ type, or the _____ type.

2. Comparatively high pressures usually require the use of a _____ instrument.

3. The oil pressure gage includes a small restriction in the inlet to prevent _____ surges from damaging the instrument.

4. When the aircraft is operated in cold-weather conditions, the tube from the oil pressure gage to the engine is filled with _____ oil.

5. All engine instruments are _____ -coded to direct attention to approaching operating difficulties.

6. Maximum and minimum allowable operating conditions are indicated on engine instruments by _____ lines.

7. When the limit and range markings are placed on the glass face of an instrument, a _____ line is placed on the glass and extended to the case of the instrument. This line is referred to as a _____ mark.

8. Diaphragm-type gages are generally used to measure comparatively _____ pressures.

9. The MAP gage is calibrated in inches of _____ . When the instrument is in standard sea-level conditions and is not on an operating engine, the reading of the instrument should be _____ inHg.

10. The purpose of a purge valve is to remove _____ from the pressure line.

11. The most critical temperature information needed for the operation of a reciprocating engine relates to _____ temperature and _____ temperature.

12. The purpose of the exhaust-gas analyzer is to indicate the _____ ratio of the mixture being burned in the cylinders.

13. The carburetor air temperature gage is important as a means of detecting _____ conditions and regulating engine performance.

14. The oil temperature gage measures the temperature of the oil _____ the engine.

15. The measurement of very high temperatures such as CHT and EGT requires the use of _____ .

16. A thermocouple is the junction of two _____ metals which generates a small electric current that varies according to the temperature of the junction.

17. The _____ is a primary engine instrument designed to provide an accurate indication of engine rpm.

18. Early tachometers were of the _____ type, employing flyweights on a rotating shaft to produce movement of the indicating needle.

19. A _____ tachometer utilizes a cylindrical magnet rotating in an aluminum drag cup to produce movement of an indicating needle.

20. An _____ tachometer involves a system that utilizes electric impulses from the magneto ignition system to produce the engine rpm indication.

21. The engine pressure ratio is the ratio of turbine _____ pressure to engine _____ pressure.

22. Gas-turbine engine tachometers are usually calibrated in _____ rpm.

23. The engine torque display indicator is known as a _____ .

24. The Fenwal continuous fire detection system utilizes a sensing element which consists of an Inconel tube with a pure _____ wire center conductor. The voids and clearances between the tubing and the conductor are saturated with a _____ mixture.

25. In the Fenwal system, at the alarm temperature of the element, the resistance of the eutectic salt drops rapidly and permits increased _____ to flow between the inner and outer conductors.

26. The sensing element of the Kidde system consists of an Inconel tube containing a _____ in which are embedded two electric conductors.

27. In the Kidde system, the resistance of the thermistor material decreases rapidly as the element is _____ .

28. Class _____ fires are those involving ordinary combustible materials such as paper, cloth, and wood.

29. Class _____ fires involve flammable liquids such as gasoline, oils, kerosene, and jet fuel.

30. Class _____ fires are those involving electrical wiring and equipment.

31. CO_2 is widely used as a fire extinguishing agent around aircraft because it can be used safely for both class _____ and class _____ fires.

32. For many aircraft fire extinguishing systems, breakable _____ disks are employed as condition indicators.

33. The rods or tubes used to transmit control lever movements are generally called _____ rods.

34. There are four types of attachment for the ends of control rods: _____ and _____ , _____ , _____ , and _____ .

35. A bellcrank is a double lever or crank arm in which there are two cranks approximately at _____ angles to each other.

36. A _____ is essentially a wheel, usually grooved, mounted in a frame or block so that it can readily turn on a fixed axis.

37. When the control handles in the cockpit reach their fore-and-aft stops just after the stops in the engine sections are reached, the control is said to be rigged with _____ .

38. A _____ push-pull control is constructed to provide for both coarse and fine adjustments.

39. The throttle knob is a thick disk that is _____ on each side.

40. The _____ control lever knob is quadrant-shaped and is scalloped on the top.

41. The mixture control lever is arranged so that a forward movement will provide a _____ mixture.

Chapter 22

Name _____

Date _____

APPLICATION QUESTIONS

1. List the three general types of mechanical engine control systems.

   a. _____

   b. _____

   c. _____

2. What type of gage is normally used to measure oil pressure? _____

3. What is the purpose of a slippage mark on an instrument?

   _____

   _____

   _____

4. Manifold pressure gages are usually what type of instruments? _____

5. Define "thermocouple."

   _____

   _____

6. What does an EPR (engine pressure ratio) gage indicate?

   _____

7. How are turbine tachometers usually calibrated or labeled? _____

8. Define the following acronyms.

   a. TGT _____

   b. EGT _____

   c. ITT _____

   d. TOT _____

   e. TIT _____

9. List four types of fire warning systems.

   a. _____

   b. _____

   c. _____

   d. _____

10. With regard to fire extinguishing systems, what does a yellow disk indicate?

    _____

11. With regard to fire extinguishing systems, what does a red disk indicate?

    _____

    _____

Chapter 22

REVIEW EXAM

1. During the inspection of an engine control system in which push-pull control rods are used, the threaded rod ends
   a. should not be adjusted in length for rigging purposes because the rod ends have been properly positioned and staked during manufacture.
   b. should be checked to determine that they are properly safetied to the push-pull rod with brass or stainless steel safety wire.
   c. should be checked for thread engagement of at least one and one-half threads but not more than three threads.
   d. should be checked for the amount of thread engagement by means of the inspection holes provided.

2. Which unit most accurately indicates fuel consumption of a reciprocating engine?
   a. Fuel flowmeter
   b. Brake mean effective pressure (bmep) indicator
   c. Fuel pressure gage
   d. Electronic fuel quantity indicator

3. The fuel flow indicator rotor and needle for a motor-impeller and turbine indicating system is driven by
   a. an electrical signal.
   b. direct coupling to the motor shaft.
   c. a friction clutch on the motor shaft.
   d. a mechanical gear train.

4. A manifold pressure gage is designed to
   a. maintain constant pressure in the intake manifold.
   b. indicate differential pressure between the intake manifold and atmospheric pressure.
   c. indicate variations of atmospheric pressure at different altitudes.
   d. indicate absolute pressure in the intake manifold.

5. Which of the following types of electric motors are commonly used in electric tachometers?
   a. Direct-current, series-wound motors
   b. Synchronous motors
   c. Direct-current, shunt-wound motors
   d. Direct-current, compound-wound motors

6. Where are the hot and cold junctions located in an engine cylinder temperature indicating system?
   a. Both junctions are located at the instrument.
   b. Both junctions are located at the cylinder.
   c. The hot junction is located at the cylinder and the cold junction is located at the instrument.
   d. The cold junction is located at the cylinder and the hot junction is located at the instrument.

7. Basically, the indicator of a tachometer system is responsive to changes in
   a. current flow.
   b. voltage polarity.
   c. frequency.
   d. voltage amplitude.

8. Which statement is correct concerning a thermo-couple-type temperature indicating instrument system?
   a. It is a balanced-type, variable resistor circuit.
   b. It requires no external power source.
   c. It usually contains a balancing circuit in the instrument case to prevent fluctuations of the system voltage from affecting the temperature reading.
   d. It will not indicate a true reading if the system voltage varies beyond the range for which it is calibrated.

9. What basic meter is used to indicate cylinder-head temperature in most aircraft?
   a. Iron-vane meter
   b. Electrodynamometer
   c. Galvanometer
   d. Thermocouple-type meter

10. Which of the following is a primary engine instrument?
    a. Tachometer
    b. Torque meter
    c. Fuel flowmeter
    d. Airspeed indicator

11. A complete break in the line between the manifold pressure gage and the induction system will be indicated by the gage registering
    a. prevailing atmospheric pressure.
    b. zero.
    c. higher than normal for prevailing conditions.
    d. lower than normal for prevailing conditions.

12. Engine oil temperature gages indicate the temperature of the oil
    a. entering the oil cooler.
    b. entering the engine.
    c. in the oil storage tank.
    d. in the return lines to the oil storage tank.

13. Consider the following statements.
    (1) Engine pressure ratio (EPR) is the ratio of the exhaust-gas pressure to the engine inlet air pressure, and indicates the thrust produced.
    (2) Engine pressure ratio (EPR) is the ratio of the exhaust-gas pressure to the engine inlet air pressure, and indicates volumetric efficiency.
    Of these two statements,

    a. only No. 1 is true.
    b. only No. 2 is true.
    c. both No. 1 and No. 2 are true.
    d. neither No. 1 nor No. 2 is true.

14. What unit in a tachometer system sends information to the indicator?
    a. The three-phase ac generator
    b. The two-phase ac generator
    c. The synchronous motor
    d. The miniature dc motor

15. The engine pressure ratio (EPR) indicator is a direct indication of
    a. the engine thrust being produced.
    b. the pressures within the turbine section.
    c. the pressure ratio between the front and aft ends of the compressor.
    d. the ratio of engine rpm to compressor pressure.

16. The exhaust-gas temperature (EGT) indicator on a gas-turbine engine provides a relative indication of the
    a. exhaust temperature.
    b. temperature of the N_1 compressor.
    c. temperature of the exhaust gases as they pass the exhaust cone.
    d. turbine inlet temperature.

17. What instrument indicates the thrust of a gas-turbine engine?
    a. Torquemeter
    b. Exhaust-gas temperature indicator
    c. Turbine inlet temperature indicator
    d. Engine pressure ratio indicator

18. In what unit of measure are turbine-engine tachometers calibrated?
    a. Percentage of engine rpm
    b. Actual engine rpm
    c. Pounds per square inch (PSI)
    d. Percentage of engine pressure ratio

19. Instruments that provide readings of low or negative pressure, such as manifold pressure gages, are usually of what type?
    a. Plenum chamber with calibrated weight
    b. Vane with calibrated spring
    c. Bourdon tube
    d. Diaphragm or bellows

20. Instruments that provide readings above approximately 10 psi, such as oil pressure gages, are usually of what type?
    a. Bimetal helix
    b. Vane with calibrated spring
    c. Bourdon tube
    d. Diaphragm or bellows

21. The EGT gage used on a reciprocating engine is primarily used to furnish temperature readings in order to
    a. obtain the best mixture setting for fuel efficiency.
    b. obtain the best mixture setting for engine cooling.
    c. prevent engine overtemperature.
    d. prevent exhaust system damage.

22. What is the function of a fire detection system?
    a. To discharge the powerplant fire extinguishing system at the origin of the fire
    b. To warn of the presence of fire in the rear section of the powerplant
    c. To activate a warning device in the event of a powerplant fire
    d. To identify the location of a powerplant fire

23. How are most aircraft turbine-engine fire extinguishing systems activated?
    a. By electrically discharged cartridges
    b. By a manual remote control valve
    c. By a piston stem and plunger
    d. By a pushrod assembly

24. A continuous-loop fire detector is what type of detector?
    a. Spot detector
    b. Overheat detector
    c. Rate-of-temperature-rise detector
    d. Radiation-sensing detector

25. What is the operating principle of the spot detector sensor in a fire detection system?
    a. Resistant core material that prevents current flow at normal temperatures
    b. Fuse material that melts at high temperature
    c. A conventional thermocouple that produces a current flow
    d. A bimetallic thermoswitch that closes when heated to a high temperature

26. Which of the following fire detection systems measures temperature rise compared to a reference temperature?
    a. Fenwal continuous loop
    b. Thermocouple
    c. Thermal switch
    d. Lindberg continuous element

27. The pulling out (or down) of an illuminated fire handle in a typical large jet aircraft fire protection system commonly accomplishes what events?
    a. Closes all firewall shutoff valves, disconnects the generator, and discharges a fire bottle
    b. Closes fuel shutoff, closes hydraulic shutoff, disconnects the generator field, and arms the fire extinguisher system
    c. Closes fuel shutoff, closes hydraulic shutoff, closes the oxygen shutoff, disconnects the generator field, and arms the fire extinguisher system
    d. Closes fuel shutoff, closes hydraulic shutoff, disconnects the generator field, extinguishes the fire warning light, and discharges the fire extinguishing system into the engine

28. The fire detection system that uses a single wire surrounded by a continuous string of ceramic beads in a tube is the
    a. Fenwal system.
    b. Lindberg system.
    c. Kidde system.
    d. thermocouple system.

29. The fire detection system that uses two wires embedded in a ceramic core within a tube is the
    a. Fenwal system.
    b. Lindberg system.
    c. thermocouple system.
    d. Kidde system.

30. A fuel or oil fire is defined as a
    a. class B fire.
    b. class D fire.
    c. class A fire.
    d. class C fire.

Answers

Chapter 1
STUDY QUESTIONS

1. single
2. even
3. one / inverted
4. 90, 60, or 45° / even
5. odd
6. five / nine
7. crankshaft
8. 14 / 18
9. cooling
10. drag
11. multiple-row radial engine
12. opposed
13. horizontal
14. a. In-line, upright
    b. In-line, inverted
    c. V type, upright
    d. V type, inverted
    e. Double-V or fan type
    f. Opposed or flat type
    g. X type
    h. Radial type, single-row
    i. Radial type, double-row
    j. Radial type, multiple-row
15. air / liquid
16. Sir Frank Whittle

Chapter 1
APPLICATION QUESTIONS

1. a. In-line
   b. Radial
   c. V-type
   d. Opposed
2. a. 3
   b. 2
   c. 1
   d. 4
   e. 10
   f. 9
   g. 7
   h. 8
   i. 5
   j. 6
3. a. Injected, opposed, 320-in³ displacement
   b. Geared, turbo, supercharged, injected, opposed, 520-in³ displacement, type of crankcase, nose section, accessory section, mode of counterweight, dual magneto
4. a. In-line type
   b. Opposed or flat type
   c. V type
   d. Single-row radial type
   e. Double-V or fan type
   f. X type
   g. Double-row radial type

Chapter 1
REVIEW EXAM

1. b
2. b
3. b
4. a
5. d

Chapter 2
STUDY QUESTIONS

1. crankcase
2. aluminum alloy
3. nose / power / fuel induction and distribution / accessory
4. bearing
5. thrust
6. plain / ball / roller
7. crankshaft
8. main journal / crankpin / crank cheek / counterweights
9. main journal
10. static balance
11. dynamic dampers
12. taper shafts / spline shafts / flange shafts
13. connecting rod
14. reciprocating / rotating
15. radial
16. knuckle pins

17. piston
18. piston rings
19. land
20. flat / recessed / concave / convex / truncated cone
21. a. To provide a seal to hold the pressures in the combustion chamber
    b. To prevent excessive oil from entering the combustion chamber
    c. To conduct the heat from the piston to the cylinder walls
22. compression / oil control
23. compression
24. oil control
25. oil wiper (or scraper)
26. piston / wrist
27. cylinder
28. barrel / head
29. nitriding
30. chokebored
31. cooling fins
32. valves
33. valve guides
34. cam
35. valve lifter
36. pushrod
37. rocker arm / stem / pushrod
38. less
39. accessory section
40. propeller

Chapter 2
APPLICATION QUESTIONS

1.

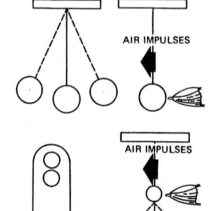

2. a. Forked-type connecting rod used on V-type engines
   b. Articulated-type connecting rod used on V-type engines
   c. Split-type connecting rod used on radial engines
   d. Solid-type connecting rod used on radial engines

3. a. Flat
   b. Recessed
   c. Cup (concave)
   d. Dome (convex)
   e. Truncated cone
4. a. Crankshaft gear
   b. Cam gear
   c. Valve lifter
   d. Pushrod
   e. Rocker arm
   f. Valve springs
   g. Valve
   h. Valve seat
5. a. Spur gear
   b. Planet gears mounted in cage attached to propeller shaft
   c. Planet-gear cage stationary
   d. Planet-gear cage drives propeller shaft

Chapter 2
REVIEW EXAM

1. b	11. a
2. d	12. b
3. c	13. d
4. d	14. c
5. b	15. d
6. c	16. b
7. b	17. c
8. a	18. d
9. a	19. d
10. a	20. c

Chapter 3
STUDY QUESTIONS

1. energy
2. inversely / constant
3. absolute temperature
4. cycle
5. intake / compression / ignition / combustion / exhaust
6. Otto
7. cylinder / piston / connecting rod / crankshaft
8. stroke
9. 180
10. Top dead center (TDC)
11. compression ratio
12. 2
13. spark plug
14. before TDC
15. compression
16. intake
17. exhaust
18. power
19. valve overlap
20. scavenging / cooling

21. valve lag
22. valve lead
23. firing order
24. Power
25. 33,000
26. piston displacement
27. indicated
28. brake
29. friction
30. manifold pressure
31. maximum except takeoff (METO) power
32. maximum
33. critical
34. thermal
35. output / input
36. volumetric
37. 100
38. temperature / pressure
39. Preignition
40. brake specific fuel consumption (bsfc)
41. power
42. economy

Chapter 3
APPLICATION QUESTIONS

1.

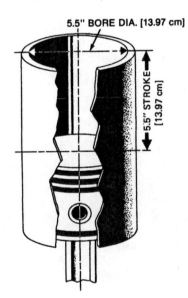

5.5" BORE DIA. [13.97 cm]

5.5" STROKE [13.97 cm]

2. 6:1
3. a. Intake
   b. Compression
   c. Power
   d. Exhaust
4. a. After bottom center
   b. After top center
   c. Before bottom center
   d. Bottom center
   e. Bottom dead center
   f. Before top center
   g. Exhaust closes
   h. Exhaust opens

i. Intake closes
j. Intake opens
k. Top center
l. Top dead center

5. a. $180° + 15° + 60° = 255°$
   b. $30°$
   c. $55° + 180° + 15° = 250°$
   d. $180° - 60° = 120°$
   e. $180° - 55° = 125°$
6. a. 542
   b. 320
   c. 846
7. a. 274
   b. 670
   c. 274
8. a. 3109
   b. 931
9. a. 0.34 / 34%
   b. 0.53 / 53%
10. a. increased
    b. increase
    c. decrease
    d. increase
    e. increase
    f. increase
11. Detonation occurs after normal ignition and is an explosion, rather than controlled burning, of the fuel. Preignition is ignition of the fuel-air mixture before the normal spark occurs.
12. 14,000
13. a. 195 hp
    b. 228 hp
14. Exhaust back pressure decreases engine performance.

Chapter 3
REVIEW EXAM

1. d
2. b
3. d
4. c
5. a
6. d
7. d
8. b
9. c
10. c
11. a
12. c
13. b
14. a
15. d
16. c
17. d
18. c
19. d
20. d
21. c
22. d
23. c
24. c
25. c

Chapter 4
STUDY QUESTIONS

1. lubricant
2. Specific gravity
3. flash point
4. viscosity
5. index
6. chemical / physical
7. sliding
8. rolling
9. dispersant
10. Multigrade / single
11. lubrication
12. pressure
13. regulator
14. bypass
15. relief valve
16. oil filter
17. full-flow
18. metal
19. separator
20. low
21. orifice
22. gear / vane
23. greater
24. wet
25. dry

Chapter 4
APPLICATION QUESTIONS

1. a. Lubrication
   b. Cooling
   c. Sealing
   d. Engine cleaning
   e. Corrosion prevention
   f. Cushioning between parts
2. A straight mineral oil is an oil that does not contain any additives except for a small amount of pour-point depressant for improved fluidity at low temperatures.
3. An ashless dispersant oil is an oil that contains a dispersant for suspending contaminants and that also contains other additives that improve the oil's antiwear and antifoaming properties. These additives are usually called "ashless" because they leave no metallic ash when they are burned up.
4. A multiviscosity oil is an oil that can provide adequate lubrication over a wider range of temperatures than can be accommodated by straight weight oils.
5. The functions of an oil pressure relief valve are to control and limit the lubricating oil pressure, to prevent damage to the lubrication system itself, and to ensure that the engine parts are not deprived of adequate lubrication.
6. A wet-sump lubrication system is one in which the oil is stored in the engine sump.

7. A dry-sump lubrication system is one in which the oil is stored in a tank outside of the engine and is pumped out of the engine and back into the tank.

Chapter 4
REVIEW EXAM

1. d	16. c
2. b	17. a
3. d	18. d
4. b	19. c
5. c	20. a
6. a	21. d
7. a	22. c
8. d	23. a
9. b	24. c
10. a	25. a
11. a	26. c
12. c	27. d
13. b	28. d
14. b	29. d
15. b	30. d

Chapter 5
STUDY QUESTIONS

1. a. the air scoop and ducting leading to the carburetor.
   b. the carburetor, or air control section, of an injection system.
   c. the intake manifold and pipes.
2. a. air scoop
   b. air filter
   c. alternate air valve
   d. carburetor air heater
3. air filter
4. wetted-type mesh / dry paper / polyurethane foam
5. alternate
6. carburetor heat
7. increases / decreases
8. impact / fuel evaporation / throttle
9. Supercharging / turbocharging
10. crankshaft / exhaust
11. turbosupercharger
12. lower
13. intake manifold
14. less
15. detonation
16. raised
17. preignition / detonation
18. internal / external
19. internal
20. external
21. exhaust
22. waste gate
23. critical
24. density / differential-pressure / exhaust bypass-valve
25. cylinders

26. baffles
27. cowl
28. conduction
29. expansion
30. shrouds

Chapter 5
APPLICATION QUESTIONS

1. a. Carburetor air box assembly
   b. Alternate air actuating arm
   c. Engine mount
   d. Carburetor heat adapter
   e. Carburetor heat shroud
   f. Left exhaust stack
   g. Propeller control conduit
   h. Conduit connector
   i. Throttle control sliding end
   j. Carburetor
   k. Alternate air control sliding end
   l. Mixture control sliding end
   m. Alternate air control conduit
   n. Right exhaust stack
   o. Vacuum line
   p. Control mounting bracket
   q. Air-oil separator line
   r. Alternate air connector
   s. Crankcase breather line
   t. Vacuum pump
   u. Air-oil separator
   v. Magnetos

2. Boyle's law expresses the relationship between pressure and volume as follows: In any sample of gas, the volume is inversely proportional to the absolute pressure if the temperature is kept constant.
3. Charles' law states that if the temperature of a given quantity of any gas is raised and the pressure is held constant, the gas will expand in proportion to the absolute temperature.
4. Engine oil pressure

Chapter 5
REVIEW EXAM

1. c	14. a
2. b	15. a
3. c	16. b
4. c	17. a
5. a	18. b
6. b	19. d
7. d	20. c
8. d	21. c
9. c	22. d
10. c	23. a
11. c	24. d
12. c	25. c
13. a	

Chapter 6
STUDY QUESTIONS

1. octane
2. lean / rich
3. TEL
4. compression ratio / manifold pressure
5. detonation
6. 150
7. boost
8. boost / engine
9. strainers
10. low / high
11. Bernoulli's
12. less / increased
13. velocity
14. mixture
15. chemically
16. 8 / 18
17. stoichiometric
18. brake specific fuel consumption
19. best-economy
20. backfire
21. propagation
22. Afterfiring
23. metering jet
24. air bleed
25. volatility / temperature / degree
26. throttle
27. level
28. main
29. idle cutoff
30. updraft
31. accelerating
32. economizer
33. mixture
34. back-suction / needle / air-port
35. automatic mixture control
36. FULL RICH
37. RICH BEST POWER
38. LEAN BEST POWER
39. downdraft
40. vaporization
41. Throttle
42. Impact
43. mass airflow
44. throttle / regulator / fuel control / discharge nozzle
45. water injection

Chapter 6
APPLICATION QUESTIONS

1. a. Point B
   b. Point B
   c. Points A and C
2. By lowering the pressure in the area of the discharge nozzle, atmospheric pressure can force the fuel out into the air stream.

3. $2C_8H_{18} + 25O_2 = 16CO_2 + 18 H_2O$
4. 0.083
5. 0.071
6. The IDLE setting
7. a. Fuel strainer
   b. Float needle valve
   c. Float
   d. Fuel level
   e. Mixture control valve
   f. Accelerator pump
   g. Idle fuel jet
   h. Power or main jet
   i. Main discharge nozzle
   j. Accelerator pump discharge nozzle
   k. Air screen
   l. Throttle valve
   m. Idle mixture control
   n. Main air bleed
   o. Economizer valve
   p. Idle air bleed
   q. Throttle
8. a. Air leak in the air intake manifold
   b. Incorrect automatic mixture control adjustment
   c. Float level too low
   d. Incorrect manual mixture control setting
   e. Clogged fuel strainer
   f. Insufficient fuel pressure
   g. Obstructed fuel line

Chapter 6
REVIEW EXAM

1.	b	16.	d
2.	c	17.	d
3.	d	18.	b
4.	a	19.	d
5.	b	20.	b
6.	b	21.	c
7.	c	22.	c
8.	c	23.	a
9.	a	24.	b
10.	b	25.	d
11.	a	26.	c
12.	c	27.	b
13.	c	28.	b
14.	c	29.	a
15.	d	30.	a

Chapter 7
STUDY QUESTIONS

1. fuel injection
2. swirl well / vapor ejector
3. intake manifold
4. air throttle / fuel control
5. LEAN

6. fuel manifold
7. cylinder head
8. fuel pressure / variable orifice
9. auxiliary
10. IDLE CUTOFF
11. air / venturi / impact
12. servo pressure regulator
13. metering jet
14. 25 / 50
15. constant head
16. air density
17. a. equal distribution
    b. shutdown
18. lean / rich
19. air-bleed
20. 180 / upward
21. IDLE CUTOFF / FULL RICH

Chapter 7
APPLICATION QUESTIONS

1. a. Freedom from vaporization icing
   b. More uniform delivery of fuel-air mixture to each cylinder
   c. Improved control of fuel-air ratio
   d. Reduction of maintenance problems
   e. Instant acceleration of engine after idling
   f. Increased engine efficiency
2. a. Fuel injection pump
   b. Fuel-air control unit
   c. Fuel manifold valve
   d. Fuel discharge nozzle
3. To meter the correct volume and pressure of fuel for all power settings and to make the pressure proportional to rpm
4. In the nozzles
5. a. Idle speed adjustment
   b. Idle mixture adjustment
   c. Idle valve
   d. Metered fuel outlet
   e. Fuel inlet strainer
   f. Inlet-fuel-pressure cap
6. a. Fuel diaphragm
   b. Air diaphragm
7. a. Impact air pressure
   b. Venturi suction
8. a. Air pressure
   b. Fuel pressure
9. a. To ensure equal distribution of metered fuel to the nozzles at and just above idle
   b. To provide isolation of each nozzle from all the others for clean engine shutdown
10. a. Plugged strainer
    b. Injector out of adjustment
    c. Faulty gage
    d. Sticky flow divider valve

Chapter 7
REVIEW EXAM

1. a
2. b
3. b
4. b
5. d

6. b
7. a
8. b
9. c
10. b

Chapter 8
STUDY QUESTIONS

1. electric spark
2. Magneto
3. alternating
4. low
5. high
6. stationary
7. magnetic / primary / secondary
8. flux linkages
9. Lenz'
10. flux / north
11. soft-iron
12. primary / secondary
13. rotating cam / magnetic field
14. capacitor / "inertia"
15. E-gap
16. turns / flux
17. one-half
18. distributor rotor
19. dual (double)
20. magneto sparking
21. coming-in
22. closed / primary
23. P-lead
24. ON
25. "hot"
26. impulse coupling
27. shower of sparks
28. primary / secondary
29. propeller
30. starter
31. open
32. one
33. pressurized
34. flashover
35. compensated cam
36. spark plug
37. air gap
38. electrodes / ceramic insulator / metal shell
39. Resistor
40. reach
41. "heat range"
42. cold / hot
43. preignition
44. fouling

Chapter 8
APPLICATION QUESTIONS

1. a. Low-tension / high-tension
   b. Rotating magnet / inductor-rotor
   c. Single / double
   d. Base-mounted / flange-mounted
2. a. Magnetic
   b. Primary
   c. Secondary
3. a. 6
   b. 1
   c. 5
   d. 2
   e. 4
   f. 7
   g. 3
4. a. Breaker contact points
   b. Breaker contact points maximum gap
   c. Condenser
   d. Rotating magneto
   e. Pole shoes
   f. Spark plug
   g. Spark plug leads
   h. Distributor
   i. Coil core
   j. Secondary winding
   k. Primary winding
   l. Ignition switch
5. a. Impulse coupling
   b. Booster coil
   c. Induction vibrator
6. To give the magneto a momentary high rotational speed and to provide a retarded spark for starting the engine
7. The vibrator current flows through the primary of the magneto coil, producing a rapidly fluctuating magnetic field around the coil. This produces a shower of sparks at the designated spark plug.
8. a. E-gap position, breaker points set to open at correct time.
   b. Magneto distributor must be timed to deliver high-tension current to proper outlet terminal of distributor block.
9. The linear distance from the shell gasket seat to the end of the shell threads (shell skirt).
10. The classification of spark plugs according to their ability to transfer heat from the firing end of the spark plug to the cylinder head.

Chapter 8
REVIEW EXAM

1. b	21. b
2. b	22. b
3. c	23. d
4. a	24. b
5. c	25. b
6. d	26. d
7. b	27. a
8. c	28. c
9. d	29. a
10. a	30. b
11. c	31. b
12. c	32. a
13. b	33. d
14. b	34. b
15. c	35. b
16. c	36. a
17. c	37. d
18. c	38. b
19. d	39. c
20. c	40. a

Chapter 9
STUDY QUESTIONS

1. OFF
2. carbon dioxide
3. eye / ear
4. ½
5. FULL INCREASE
6. COLD (off)
7. FULL RICH
8. IDLE CUTOFF
9. ⅛ / FULL RICH / IDLE CUTOFF
10. FULL RICH
11. 30 / 60 / shut off
12. liquid lock
13. 50 / 125
14. HIGH-RPM (low-pitch)
15. cycled
16. cylinder head temperatures (CHTs)
17. cylinder head
18. MAP / rpm / rpm / MAP
19. clear the engine
20. cruise
21. HEAT ON
22. IDLE CUTOFF
23. spark plug fouling
24. fuel / water / contaminants
25. Preheating
26. 43 / D
27. metal

28. compression
29. direct-compression / differential-pressure
30. 25
31. valves
32. welded / clamped
33. exhaust / cracks
34. dyna-focal
35. Troubleshooting
36. piston rings
37. Backfiring
38. Afterfiring

Chapter 9
APPLICATION QUESTIONS

1. a. Set the master switch to ON.
   b. Turn on the boost pump if needed.
   c. Open the throttle approximately 1/2 in (0.127 cm).
   d. If the engine is equipped with a constant-speed propeller, set the propeller control at the FULL INCREASE position.
   e. Set the mixture lever at the FULL RICH position.
   f. Clear the propeller.
   g. Turn the ignition switch to the START position.
   h. Release the ignition switch.
   i. Check for oil pressure.
2. a. Engine oil pressure
   b. Oil temperature
   c. Cylinder-head temperature (CHT)
   d. Engine rpm
   e. Manifold pressure
   f. Drop in rpm during switching to single-magneto operation.
   g. Engine response to propeller controls, if a constant-speed (controllable-pitch) propeller is used.
   h. Exhaust-gas temperature (EGT).
3. Leaning saves on fuel and prevents the spark plugs from being fouled, providing for better engine operation.
4. 80 psi
5. 25 percent
6. a. Dry paper filter
   b. Wire-mesh wetted oil-type filter
   c. Foam-type filter
7. a. Symptom recognition
   b. Symptom elaboration
   c. Listing of probable faulty functions
   d. Localizing the fault
   e. Isolating the fault to a component
   f. Failure analysis
8. a. Lack of fuel
   b. Engine overprimed
   c. Induction system leakage
   d. Starter slippage

Chapter 9
REVIEW EXAM

1. b
2. d
3. a
4. d
5. a
6. b
7. d
8. d
9. d
10. a
11. c
12. d
13. b
14. b
15. d
16. d
17. c
18. c
19. a
20. d

Chapter 10
STUDY QUESTIONS

1. manufacturer
2. top
3. operation
4. overhauled
5. rebuilt
6. zero time
7. manufacturer / manufacturer
8. integral / propeller
9. overhaul
10. certificated repair station
11. receiving
12. conforms
13. service bulletins
14. Airworthiness Directives
15. Table of Limits
16. disassembly
17. magnifying glass
18. abrasion
19. crack
20. fretting
21. gouging
22. oxidation
23. scoring
24. degreasing / decarbonizing
25. structural
26. ferromagnetic
27. electric current
28. permeability
29. liquid penetrant
30. Ultrasonic
31. eddy-current
32. Dimensional
33. bore gage
34. thickness
35. dial indicator
36. grinding
37. interference fit
38. preignition
39. lapped
40. cast iron / steel
41. honing
42. smaller
43. Heli-Coil
44. a. Pistons
    b. Piston pins
    c. Piston rings
    d. Exhaust valves
    e. Valve keepers
    f. Main and rod bearings; all bushings
    g. Connecting-rod bolts and nuts
    h. All hoses, gaskets, seals, cotter pins, circlips, lock plates, and retaining rings
45. torque
46. pre-oiled
47. corrosion

Chapter 10
APPLICATION QUESTIONS

1. a. Receiving inspection
   b. Disassembly
   c. Visual inspection
   d. Cleaning
   e. Structural inspection
   f. Dimensional inspection
   g. Repair and replacement
   h. Reassembly
   i. Installation
   j. Engine testing and run-in
   k. Preservation and storage
2. The wear caused by two parts rubbing together under light pressure and without lubrication.
3. The surface erosion caused by very slight movement between two surfaces which are tightly pressed together.
4. The severe erosion of metal between two surfaces which are pressed tightly together and moved one against the other. Galling can be considered a severe form of fretting.
5. Deep scratches or grooves caused by hard particles between moving surfaces.
6. a. The person stripping the engine parts must be careful to follow the instructions of the manufacturer of the stripping agent and the manufacturer of the engine.
   b. Dissimilar metals should not be placed in the solution tank at the same time.
   c. Immersion times should be carefully observed.
   d. It is inadvisable to soak aluminum and magnesium parts in solutions containing soap.
   e. Steel parts that have been washed with soap and water should be coated with a rust-inhibiting oil immediately after the cleaning operation is completed.

f. Care must be exercised in the handling of decarbonizing solutions to prevent the material from contacting the skin, because these solutions will usually cause severe irritation or burning. The operator should wear goggles, rubber gloves, and protective clothing while working with these solutions.

7. Circular magnetization is achieved by passing the current directly through the part.

8. Longitudinal magnetization is accomplished by wrapping heavy-gage wire around the part, or by placing the part in the magnetizing coil.

9. To determine the degree of wear for parts of the engine where moving surfaces are in contact with other surfaces.

10. Grinding wheel
11. One
12. Green
13. 66.7
14. 80
15. 2800 rpm for 10 minutes

Chapter 10
REVIEW EXAM

1. a	9. c
2. d	10. b
3. c	11. d
4. c	12. c
5. b	13. d
6. b	14. c
7. b	15. a
8. c	

Chapter 11
STUDY QUESTIONS

1. turbojet
2. mass / accelerated
3. directly proportional
4. force / mass
5. ram
6. air compressor / combustion section / turbine section
7. turbojet / turbofan / turboprop / turboshaft
8. hot gases
9. turbofan
10. high / low
11. low / high
12. "ducted fan"
13. turboprop
14. turboshaft
15. velocity
16. weight
17. Boyle's
18. Charles'
19. Thrust
20. Density
21. decrease
22. up
23. slight
24. negligible
25. water
26. cools / pressure
27. output / input
28. thrust specific fuel consumption
29. jet nozzle
30. Cycle
31. Combustion
32. Thermal
33. inlet guide
34. centrifugal / axial
35. discharge / inlet
36. impeller / diffuser / compressor manifold
37. centrifugal
38. rotor / stator
39. turbine
40. low / high
41. ratio
42. compressor stall
43. diffuser
44. velocity
45. cooling
46. annular / can
47. nozzle diaphragm
48. highest
49. impulse / reaction / reaction-impulse
50. reaction
51. "fir tree" / "dovetail"
52. "choked" / temperature
53. cool / hot
54. velocity / temperature
55. fuel
56. temperature / thrust
57. aerodynamic blockage / mechanical blockage
58. accessory drive
59. decibels
60. frequencies

Chapter 11
APPLICATION QUESTIONS

1. John Barber
2. Heinkel Aircraft Company
3. August 27, 1939
4. a. Rocket
   b. Ram jet
   c. Pulse jet
   d. Gas turbine
5. a. Turbojet
   b. Turbofan
   c. High-bypass turbofan
   d. Turboprop
   e. Turboshaft
6. a. A body at rest tends to remain at rest, and a body in motion tends to continue in motion in a straight line, unless caused to change its state by an external force.

b. The acceleration of a body is directly proportional to the force causing it and inversely proportional to the mass of the body.

c. For every action, there is an equal and opposite reaction.

7. a. Decrease
   b. Increase

8. a. Increase
   b. Decrease

9. $F = \dfrac{W_a}{g}(V_2 - V_1)$

10. 279.7

11. 248.59

12. 222.98

13. Decrease

14. The amount of thrust developed by the jet nozzle compared with the energy supplied to it in a usable form.

15. a. Centrifugal type
    b. Axial type

16. The failure of the compressor blades to move the air at the designed flow rate. When this occurs, the air velocity in the first compressor stage is reduced to a level at which the angle of attack of the compressor blades reaches a stall value.

17. a. Can
    b. Can-annular or cannular
    c. Annular

18. a. Impulse
    b. Reaction
    c. Reaction-impulse

19. The pressure and speed of the gases passing through the impulse section of the turbine blades remain essentially the same, the only change being in the direction of flow. The reaction section of the turbine blades changes the speed and pressure of the gases. As the gases pass between the turbine blades, the cross-sectional area of the passage decreases and causes an increase in gas velocity.

20. a. Fir-tree slots
    b. Dovetail slots

21. To assist the brake system in slowing the aircraft after landing.

22. Any two of the following: Electrostream drilling; Electric-discharge machining; Laser drilling; Laser-beam welding

Chapter 11
REVIEW EXAM

1. d	10. d
2. c	11. c
3. b	12. b
4. a	13. d
5. b	14. a
6. b	15. b
7. c	16. c
8. a	17. b
9. b	18. c

19. a	25. b
20. c	26. a
21. c	27. a
22. c	28. d
23. a	29. c
24. a	30. d

Chapter 12
STUDY QUESTIONS

1. kerosene / wide-cut
2. higher
3. low
4. low
5. more
6. a. fuel tanks
   b. fuel boost pumps
   c. fuel shutoff valve
   d. low-pressure fuel filter
7. a. main fuel pump
   b. fuel filter
   c. main engine control
   d. oil cooler
   e. flow divider
   f. fuel nozzles
8. spray nozzles
9. bypass valve
10. duplex
11. air spray
12. rich
13. lean
14. a. ambient pressure
    b. CIT
    c. burner pressure
    d. high-pressure compressor (N_2) rotor speed
    e. power lever (throttle) position
15. hydromechanical
16. combustion
17. discharge
18. metered
19. N_g / power lever
20. fuel
21. a. pressure-regulating valve sensor
    b. pressure-regulating valve
    c. throttle valve
22. servo
23. speed governor / actual / desired
24. stator vanes / inlet
25. stalling
26. a. engine speed
    b. compressor inlet temperature (CIT)
    c. compressor discharge pressure (CDP)
    d. power lever position
27. variable
28. on-speed
29. servo piston
30. supervisory
31. full-authority

Chapter 12
APPLICATION QUESTIONS

1. a. Be pumpable and flow easily under all operating conditions
   b. Permit engine starting at all ground conditions and give satisfactory flight relighting characteristics
   c. Provide efficient combustion at all conditions
   d. Have as high a calorific (heat) value as possible
   e. Produce minimal harmful effects on the combustion system or turbine blades
   f. Produce minimal corrosive effects on fuel system components
   g. Provide adequate lubrication for the moving parts of the fuel system
   h. Reduce fire hazards to a minimum
2. a. Jet A
   b. Jet B
3. a. Fuel icing or gelling
   b. Microorganisms
4. A duplex nozzle requires a primary and a main fuel manifold and has two independent orifices, one much smaller than the other.
5. a. Engine speed
   b. Throttle position
   c. Compressor inlet temperature
   d. Compressor discharge pressure
   e. Exhaust-gas temperature
6. The full-authority EEC system performs all functions necessary to operate a turbofan engine efficiently and safely in all modes, such as starting, accelerating, decelerating, takeoff, climb, cruise, and idle.

Chapter 12
REVIEW EXAM

1. b
2. b
3. d
4. c
5. b
6. d
7. a
8. c
9. c
10. a

Chapter 13
STUDY QUESTIONS

1. synthetic
2. solvent
3. type / grade
4. gear
5. dry-sump
6. Scavenge
7. higher
8. microns
9. magnetic chip
10. fuel / air
11. breather
12. pressure relief valve / full-flow / total-loss
13. pressure relief valve
14. full-flow
15. total-loss
16. analysis
17. atomic absorption / optical emission spectrometry

Chapter 13
APPLICATION QUESTIONS

1. Synthetic
2. a. Pressure relief valve system
   b. Full-flow system
   c. Total-loss system
3. A magnetic chip detector is a device that indicates the presence of metal contamination without requiring that the filter be opened.
4. A labyrinth-type seal is a seal that undergoes virtually no wear because its rotating and stationary members do not touch. There are two seal chambers: the oil seal next to the bearing forms one chamber, and the air seal forms a pressurized chamber between itself and the oil seal. The oil seal must retain the oil in the sump with the aid of the air seal. Oil for lubrication of the bearing flows through the oil jet, over the bearing, and out through the oil drain.
5. A developing engine problem.

Chapter 13
REVIEW EXAM

1. a
2. d
3. a
4. a
5. d
6. a
7. d
8. c
9. d
10. c
11. c
12. b
13. d
14. c
15. c

Chapter 14
STUDY QUESTIONS

1. exciter box / ignition lead / igniter
2. ignition lead
3. combustion
4. electrodes / fuel
5. starting
6. high-energy
7. capacitor discharge
8. flameout
9. glow plug
10. insulators / electrodes / shell body / internal seals
11. continuous / low-intensity
12. snapping
13. low
14. air-turbine
15. low-pressure / high pressure
16. high / low
17. gas-turbine / cartridge-type
18. gas-turbine

Chapter 14
APPLICATION QUESTIONS

1. During starting or continuous ignition
2. a. Ignition exciter unit
   b. High-tension igniter output leads
   c. Spark igniter
3. A device, such as a spark plug, used to start the burning of the air-fuel mixture in a combustion chamber
4. 30 seconds
5. a. Electric
   b. Air-turbine
6. Compressed air
7. a. Cross feed from running engine
   b. APU (auxiliary power unit)
   c. Ground start (air cart) supply
8. A compact, self-contained gas-turbine engine which provides compressed air and aircraft electric power.
9. a. Electrical power
   b. Compressed air

Chapter 14
REVIEW EXAM

1. d
2. d
3. b
4. a
5. c
6. c
7. d
8. a
9. d
10. c

Chapter 15
STUDY QUESTIONS

1. twin / axial
2. air inlet / compressor / combustion / turbine / exhaust / accessory / fan discharge
3. air inlet
4. inlet guide
5. two
6. weight
7. inner
8. first
9. loss of air
10. pressure
11. decreases / velocity
12. 4 / 7
13. losses
14. fir-tree
15. five
16. twin / four
17. two
18. fan / low-pressure (N_1) compressor / high-pressure (N_2) compressor / high-compressor drive-turbine / low-compressor drive-turbine
19. low / high
20. unison
21. annular
22. twin / axial
23. five / two
24. turbine / turbine
25. three
26. cowl / dome / inner / outer
27. two
28. three / fan / core / low-pressure turbine
29. three
30. fan / intermediate
31. inside
32. first / outermost
33. 18
34. impingement
35. reduction gear
36. low
37. four / three
38. centrifugal / axial
39. three
40. 180 / high
41. reverse
42. modular

Chapter 15
APPLICATION QUESTIONS

1. a. Boeing 727
   b. Boeing 737
   c. DC-9
2. 200 series
3. Two
4. a. Boeing 767
   b. Boeing 747-300
   c. Airbus A310
5. 37,000 lb
6. 50,000 to 60,000 lb
7. a. CF6-6
   b. CF6-50
   c. CF6-80
8. a. Boeing 767
   b. Airbus Industrie A310
9. Three
10. Fan reduction gearbox
11. Annular reverse-flow

Chapter 15
REVIEW EXAM

1. c
2. a
3. d
4. c
5. c
6. d
7. a
8. c
9. c
10. a
11. d
12. d
13. a
14. c
15. c

Chapter 16
STUDY QUESTIONS

1. turboprop
2. generator / producer
3. power turbine
4. free
5. fixed
6. higher
7. propeller
8. single / two / can / three
9. pressure / flame
10. air
11. compressor
12. reverse
13. power / condition / hydromechanical / electronic
14. torque / electronic
15. pitch-change
16. single / five / centrifugal / annular / two / free
17. accessory / cold / hot / power-turbine
18. overspeed / ground / takeoff / propeller speed / torque / temperature
19. constant-speed / beta
20. MAX REVERSE / FLIGHT IDLE
21. free
22. foreign objects
23. axial / three / centrifugal
24. compressor / combustion
25. reverse / annular
26. cooling
27. single
28. opposite / compressor / propeller
29. counterclockwise
30. shroud
31. interstage baffle
32. clockwise
33. propeller / 15:1
34. torquemeter
35. power
36. compressor / bearing compartment / turbine disk
37. compressor
38. oil
39. glow
40. compressor / turbine
41. centrifugal
42. three / compressor / propeller
43. feathers

Chapter 16
APPLICATION QUESTIONS

1. In this engine, the turbine is not mechanically connected to the gas generator; instead, an additional turbine wheel is placed in the exhaust stream from the gas generator.
2. In this engine, the shaft is mechanically connected to the gearbox so that the high-speed, low-torque rota-

tional energy transmitted to the gearbox from the turbine can then be converted to the low-speed, high-torque power required to drive the propeller.
3. a. Compressor section
   b. Combustion section
   c. Turbine section
4. Gas generator
5. Single-spool gas generator section consisting of a five-stage axial compressor and a single-stage centrifugal flow compressor: a low-fuel-pressure through-flow annular combustion chamber; an air-cooled, two-stage, axial-flow high-pressure turbine; and a free, two-stage, uncooled axial-flow power turbine.
6. a. Power lever
   b. Condition lever
7. Free-turbine
8. a. Beech King Air
   b. Twin Otter
9. a. Propeller reduction gearbox
   b. Power-turbine support housing
   c. Exhaust duct
   d. Power turbine
   e. Compressor turbine
   f. Combustion-chamber liner
   g. Fuel manifold
   h. Gas generator case
   i. Compressor bleed valve
   j. Compressor assembly
   k. Compressor inlet case
   l. Oil-to-fuel heater
   m. Dipstick and filler cap
   n. Accessory gearbox
   o. Ignition-current regulator
   p. Fuel-control unit and pump
   q. Air inlet screen
   r. Ignition glow plug
   s. Compressor-turbine guide vanes
   t. Power-turbine guide vanes
10. Two
11. Centrifugal
12. Three

Chapter 16
REVIEW EXAM

1. c   6. c
2. c   7. d
3. d   8. c
4. a   9. d
5. c   10. c

Chapter 17
STUDY QUESTIONS

1. turboshaft
2. shaft horsepower
3. auxiliary power units

4. 100
5. power section / load compressor / gearbox
6. shaft
7. compressed air
8. power
9. 7 / 95
10. free / helicopter
11. five / one / two / two
12. compressor / power
13. pressure / combustor
14. reversed
15. air-inlet
16. compressor
17. acceleration / deceleration
18. reduction-gear
19. oil
20. compressor / turbine / combustion / accessory gearbox
21. front / rear / center
22. two / two
23. reduction-gear
24. 6016
25. dry
26. freewheeling
27. no / no
28. free
29. Autorotation

Chapter 17
APPLICATION QUESTIONS

1. a. Model 250-C20B/F/J
   b. Model 250-C28B
   c. Model 250-C28C
   d. Model 250-C30/P/R
2. a. Fuel pump
   b. Gas-producer fuel control
   c. Power-turbine governor
   d. Fuel nozzle
3. Shaft horsepower
4. Engine oil

Chapter 17
REVIEW EXAM

1. b
2. b
3. b
4. b
5. c
6. a
7. b
8. a
9. a
10. b
11. c
12. d

Chapter 18
STUDY QUESTIONS

1. foreign-object
2. generators
3. air-turbine
4. hot
5. false / hung
6. flight
7. periodic
8. special
9. fiberscope
10. Foreign-object
11. overlapping
12. EGT
13. rotating
14. hot section
15. time-in-service / on-condition
16. Maintenance
17. Scheduled
18. Unscheduled
19. line
20. starter
21. leakage / functional
22. pattern
23. compressor wash
24. time before overhaul
25. "on condition"
26. rotating
27. dry motoring
28. wet motoring
29. power assurance
30. trimming
31. Troubleshooting
32. Fault
33. trend analysis

Chapter 18
APPLICATION QUESTIONS

1. Internal engine damage, ranging from small nicks and scratches to complete disablement or destruction of the engine, resulting from ingestion of foreign objects
2. a. Rotation of the engine at a speed sufficient to provide adequate air volume and velocity
   b. Provision of high-intensity ignition
   c. Introduction of fuel through the fuel nozzles
3. A radius of 25 ft
4. A hot start
5. A hung start or false start
6. An attempt to ignite the fuel before the engine has been accelerated sufficiently by the starter
7. Air-turbine starter
8. a. Fill oil tanks. Enter in the inspection records the number of quarts added for each engine.
   b. Service the constant-speed drive as required.
   c. Check engine inlet, cowling, and pylon for damage. Check for irregularities and exterior leakage.
   d. Inspect the engine exhaust section for damage using a strong inspection light. Note condition of rear turbine.

e. Check the thrust-reverser ejectors and reverser buckets for security and damage.

f. Check the reverser system, with ejectors extended, for cracks, buckling, and damage.

9. a. Borescope
    b. Fiberscope
    c. Videoscope

10. Maintenance in which checks are carried out progressively and as convenient within given time limits, rather than at specific aircraft check periods

11. a. Ambient air temperature (T_{am})
    b. Ambient air pressure (P_{am})
    c. Exhaust total pressure (P_{t7})
    d. N_1 rpm
    e. N_2 rpm
    f. Exhaust-gas temperature (EGT)
    g. Fuel flow pounds (W_f), lb/h (pph)
    h. Thrust (F_a)
    i. Low-pressure compressor outlet pressure (P_{s3})
    j. High-pressure compressor outlet pressure (P_{s4})

12. 1.007

13. 1.03

14. 90.6

15. 420 lb/h

16. To make sure that the engine will achieve takeoff power on a hot day without exceeding rpm and temperature limitations

17. To give an indication of any engine deterioration at the earliest possible stage and also to help identify any area or module in which deterioration is occurring

Chapter 18
REVIEW EXAM

1.	b	19.	b
2.	a	20.	c
3.	b	21.	c
4.	c	22.	c
5.	d	23.	d
6.	a	24.	d
7.	d	25.	c
8.	c	26.	b
9.	a	27.	c
10.	d	28.	d
11.	d	29.	b
12.	c	30.	c
13.	b	31.	a
14.	d	32.	b
15.	d	33.	b
16.	d	34.	d
17.	c	35.	b
18.	b		

Chapter 19
STUDY QUESTIONS

1. rotating
2. thrust
3. crankshaft
4. geared
5. blade-element / Dryewiecki
6. angle of attack
7. third
8. true
9. stations
10. blade
11. pitch
12. relative
13. effective
14. geometrical
15. slip
16. diameter
17. zero-thrust
18. thrust
19. Centrifugal
20. opposite
21. Thrust
22. high
23. low
24. thrust
25. efficiency
26. 1
27. tractor
28. Pusher
29. fixed
30. ground
31. controllable
32. aerodynamic
33. governor
34. "feathering"
35. "windmill"
36. negative
37. aerodynamic
38. aluminum
39. counterweight forces / spring forces / centrifugal twisting moments / nitrogen
40. oil
41. flyweights
42. increase
43. reduce / increase
44. increase / feather
45. lower / oil
46. isopropyl alcohol
47. electric
48. synchronization
49. synchrophasing

Chapter 19
APPLICATION QUESTIONS

1. The angle between the face or chord of a particular blade section and the plane in which the propeller blades rotate.
2. Designated distances measured in inches along the blade as measured from the center of the hub.
3. See art at bottom of page.
4. 68.58 pitch inches
5. a. Centrifugal force
   b. Torque bending force
   c. Thrust bending force
   d. Aerodynamic twisting force
   e. Centrifugal twisting force
6. a. Tricycle landing gear, 7 in; tail-wheel landing gear, 9 in
   b. 18 in
   c. Radial, 1 in; longitudinal, 1/2 in
7. a. Tractor propellers
   b. Pusher propellers
8. a. Fixed-pitch
   b. Ground-adjustable
   c. Controllable-pitch
   d. Two-position pitch
   e. Constant-speed
   f. Automatic-pitch
9. Feathering consists of changing the pitch of the propeller to an angle at which forward aircraft motion produces a minimum windmilling effect on a "power-off" propeller.
10. To minimize drag from the propeller during an engine loss or engine out
11. a. On-speed
    b. Underspeed
    c. Overspeed
12. a. Counterweight forces
    b. Spring forces
    c. Centrifugal twisting moments (CTMs)
    d. Air/nitrogen charges
13. Governor oil pressure
14. Overspeed
15. On-speed
16. Underspeed
17. a. Anti-icing (alcohol)
    b. Deicing (electrical)
18. To reduce vibration and noise

Chapter 19
REVIEW EXAM

1. b	21. a
2. d	22. a
3. c	23. b
4. b	24. c
5. c	25. c
6. a	26. b
7. b	27. a
8. a	28. c
9. a	29. b
10. a	30. c
11. d	31. b
12. a	32. c
13. d	33. d
14. b	34. d
15. d	35. c
16. d	36. b
17. b	37. d
18. b	38. b
19. a	39. d
20. c	40. d

Chapter 20
STUDY QUESTIONS

1. shaft
2. net thrust
3. equivalent shaft
4. rotation
5. feathering
6. reduced
7. increases
8. beta
9. oil / spring / counterweight
10. low
11. in-flight / ground

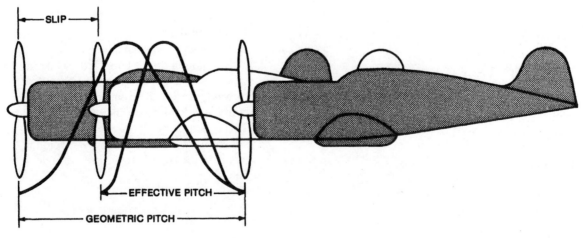

12. negative torque
13. low / high
14. a. Significant weight reduction
    b. Improved repairability
    c. Damage tolerance
    d. Vibration damping
    e. Design flexibility
15. centrifugal / bending / torsional
16. lightning
17. overspeed
18. fuel
19. fuel / power / propeller
20. CUTOFF / IDLE
21. feather
22. angle
23. decreases
24. constant
25. underspeed
26. overspeed
27. FLIGHT IDLE
28. 106
29. reverse
30. LOW PITCH / REVERSE PITCH / HIGH PITCH / FEATHER
31. fuel / engine
32. power
33. beta
34. spring / flyweight
35. blade angle / engine speed
36. feather
37. low
38. 82 / 104
39. coordinator
40. beta
41. condition / power
42. power-turbine / beta control
43. constant-speed / beta
44. constant-speed / beta

Chapter 20
APPLICATION QUESTIONS

1. shp = prop speed (rpm) × torque (ft • lb) × 0.00019
2. 342 horsepower
3. 755 horsepower
4. It is much lighter.
5. a. Condition lever
   b. Power control lever
   c. Propeller control lever
6. To prevent the propeller from going into reverse pitch during normal flight
7. Beta ring
8. a. Propeller governor
   b. Underspeed governor
   c. Propeller pitch control
   d. Feathering valve

Chapter 20
REVIEW EXAM

1.	d	6.	d
2.	c	7.	c
3.	c	8.	a
4.	d	9.	c
5.	b	10.	d

Chapter 21
STUDY QUESTIONS

1. crankshaft
2. Flange
3. two / eight
4. Prussian blue
5. dry air / nitrogen gas
6. feathering
7. crankshaft / oil
8. first flight / 25
9. one
10. plane
11. major
12. minor
13. major
14. minor
15. 65
16. visual / magnetic
17. bent / cracked / dented
18. fatigue
19. tip
20. debond
21. Delamination
22. distortion
23. gouge
24. split
25. fatigue
26. universal propeller protractor
27. static
28. Type Certificate Data Sheet
29. fixed

Chapter 21
APPLICATION QUESTIONS

1. a. Tapered shaft
   b. Splined shaft
   c. Flange-type crankshaft
2. This condition can be corrected by inserting a longer spacer, which moves the entire propeller assembly forward, causing the front cone to seat in the hub before its apex hits the end of the shaft spline.
3. This condition can be corrected by carefully removing not more than 1/16 in of material from the front edge (apex) of the cone or replacing the cone with a new one.

4. a. Spinner cap attachment screw
   b. Spinner cap
   c. Air valve
   d. Check nut
   e. Low pitch stop
   f. O-ring
   g. Spinner
   h. Spinner attachment screw
   i. Check nut
   j. Hub bolt
   k. Hub nut
   l. Blade
   m. Aft spinner bulkhead
   n. Stud
   o. O-ring
   p. Shim
   q. Thimble
   r. Spring
   s. Sleeve
   t. Starter ring gear
5. To ensure that all blades of a propeller are rotating in the same plane of rotation
6. a. Horizontal position
   b. Vertical position
7. Airworthy damage does not affect flight safety characteristics of the blades, although areas of minor damage should be repaired to maintain aerodynamic efficiency.
8. To check for debond and delamination
9. To ensure that the engine is developing its rated power

Chapter 21
REVIEW EXAM

1. b
2. b
3. a
4. a
5. d
6. d
7. a
8. a
9. d
10. c
11. d
12. d
13. a
14. b
15. d

Chapter 22
STUDY QUESTIONS

1. bourdon-tube / diaphragm / bellows
2. bourdon-tube
3. pressure
4. light
5. color
6. red
7. white / slippage
8. low
9. mercury / 29.92 [101.34 kPa]
10. moisture
11. oil / cylinder-head
12. fuel-air
13. icing
14. entering
15. thermocouples
16. dissimilar
17. tachometer
18. mechanical
19. magnetic
20. electronic
21. discharge / inlet
22. percent
23. torquemeter
24. nickel / eutectic salt
25. current
26. thermistor
27. heated
28. A
29. B
30. C
31. B / C
32. colored
33. push-pull
34. clevis / pin / ball bearing / ball joint / threaded
35. right
36. pulley
37. "springback"
38. vernier
39. flat
40. propeller
41. richer

Chapter 22
APPLICATION QUESTIONS

1. a. Push-pull rods
   b. Cable and pulley systems
   c. Flexible push-pull wires encased in coiled-wire sheathing
2. Bourdon tube
3. The slippage mark will be broken and offset if the cover glass should move. When this condition is noted, the cover glass should be rotated until the white line is again in alignment.
4. Diaphragm type
5. The junction of two dissimilar metals which generates a small electric current that varies according to the temperature of the junction

6. The thrust developed by the engine
7. Percent rpm
8. a. Turbine-gas temperature
   b. Exhaust-gas temperature
   c. Interturbine temperature
   d. Turbine outlet temperature
   e. Turbine inlet temperature
9. a. Thermocouple
   b. Fenwal continuous loop
   c. Kidde
   d. Pneumatic system (Donner)
10. That an extinguishing agent has been discharged by use of the cockpit controls
11. That discharge has occurred as a result of overpressure and rupture of the safety disk in the outlet of the agent container

Chapter 22
REVIEW EXAM

1. d		16. d
2. a		17. d
3. a		18. a
4. d		19. d
5. b		20. c
6. c		21. a
7. c		22. c
8. b		23. a
9. c		24. b
10. a		25. a
11. a		26. b
12. b		27. b
13. a		28. a
14. a		29. d
15. a		30. a